Ron McManus, DMin, PhD
Glen Jennings, EdD
Editors

Structured Exercises for Promoting Family and Group Strengths: A Handbook for Group Leaders, Trainers, Educators, Counselors, and Therapists

Pre-publication
REVIEWS,
COMMENTARIES,
EVALUATIONS . . .

"**I**t is widely accepted today that human relations, knowledge, and skills are best learned experientially. Family life educators, counselors, therapists, and group leaders of all kinds are constantly searching for good exercises to help individuals, groups, and families make lasting change. *Structured Exercises for Promoting Family and Group Strengths* is an excellent reference source for such exercises.

Ease of use is a major criteria in the selection of any reference book. This book is extremely easy to read. Exercises are divided into six convenient sections–Icebreakers, Assessors, Dyad/Couples Discussion Starters, Group/Family Discussions, Enhancers, and Energizers. These sections make it easy to find the type of exercise you want quickly. Selection is made even easier by a four to five sentence description of each exercise at the beginning of each section. Use of the exercises is facilitated by a common format which provides essential information–objectives, materials needed, time required, and clear, specific procedures–for implementing each exercise. This is a volume that will be used frequently and will have a special place on the book shelf."

Preston M. Dyer, PhD
Professor of Sociology
and Social Work,
Director, Social Work Division,
Baylor University

The Haworth Press, Inc.

Structured Exercises for Promoting Family and Group Strengths

A Handbook for Group Leaders, Trainers, Educators, Counselors, and Therapists

HAWORTH Marriage & the Family
Terry S. Trepper, PhD
Senior Editor

Christiantown, USA by Richard Stellway

Marriage and Family Therapy: A Sociocognitive Approach by Nathan Hurvitz and Roger A. Straus

Culture and Family: Problems and Therapy by Wen-Shing Tseng and Jing Hsu

Adolescents and Their Families: An Introduction to Assessment and Intervention by Mark Worden

Parents Whose Parents Were Divorced by R. Thomas Berner

The Effect of Children on Parents by Anne-Marie Ambert

Multigenerational Family Therapy by David S. Freeman

101 Interventions in Family Therapy edited by Thorana S. Nelson and Terry S. Trepper

Therapy with Treatment Resistant Families: A Consultation-Crisis Intervention Model by William George McCown, Judith Johnson, and Associates

The Death of Intimacy: Barriers to Meaningful Interpersonal Relationships by Philip M. Brown

Developing Healthy Stepfamilies: Twenty Families Tell Their Stories by Patricia Kelley

Propagations: Thirty Years of Influence from the Mental Research Institute edited by John H. Weakland and Wendel A. Ray

Structured Exercises for Promoting Family and Group Strengths: A Handbook for Group Leaders, Trainers, Educators, Counselors, and Therapists edited by Ron McManus and Glen Jennings

Structured Exercises for Promoting Family and Group Strengths

A Handbook for Group Leaders, Trainers, Educators, Counselors, and Therapists

Ron McManus, DMin, PhD
Glen Jennings, EdD
Editors

The Haworth Press
New York • London

The Haworth Press, Inc., 10 Alice Street, Binghamton, NY 13904-1580

Paperback edition published in 1997.

Cover design by Stephanie Torta

Library of Congress Cataloging-in-Publication Data

McManus, Ron.

    Structured exercises for promoting family and group strengths : a handbook for group leaders, trainers, educators, counselors and therapists / by Ron McManus and Glen Jennings.
       p. cm.
    Includes index.
    ISBN 0-7890-0224-8 (alk. paper)
    1. Group psychotherapy–Problems, exercises, etc. 2. Group relations training–Problems, exercises, etc. 3. Family psychotherapy–Problems, exercises, etc. I. Jennings, Glen. II. Title.
RC488.M37 1995
616.89'15–dc20
                                                   95-4829
                                                    CIP

CONTENTS

ABOUT THE EDITORS

Ron McManus, DMin, PhD, is Professor of Religion and Psychology at Texas Wesleyan University. He has also served as a lecturer in bioethics in the Department of Medical Humanities at Texas College of Osteopathic Medicine. He has published work in the areas of family therapy, therapeutic games, and medical ethics. Dr. McManus is a Licensed Professional Counselor, a Licensed Chemical Dependency Counselor, a Licensed Marriage and Family Therapist, and a supervisor of the American Association for Marriage and Family Therapy. He holds a masters degree in theology and doctorates in the areas of pastoral counseling and marriage and family therapy.

Glen H. Jennings, EdD, is Professor of Family Sciences at Texas Woman's University. He is a guest lecturer at the California Family Study Center and a consulting faculty member for the Saybrook Institute. He has published in journals and chapters in books and has worked with Ron McManus developing therapeutic games. He is a member of the American Counseling Association, the International Association for Marriage and Family Counseling, the Association for Specialists in Group Work, the Society for the Scientific Study of Sex, and the National Council on Family Relations. He holds a doctorate in child development and family relations from Oklahoma State University.

List of Contributors

Peggy Avent, PhD, Licensed Professional Counselor and Licensed Family Therapist, Centerpoint Institute for Human Development, San Antonio, TX.

Linda J. Brock, MS, Sexuality Educator with Snyder & Associates of Denton and Lewisville, TX.

Mary Jane Clayborn, MS, Counselor, Arlington, TX.

Dixie Dibley, MS, Counselor, Burleson, TX.

Stephen Freeman, PhD, Licensed Professional Counselor, Carrollton, TX; Professor of Counseling and Development at Texas Woman's University.

Lee Hipple, MSW, Professor of Social Work, Texas Woman's University; Jester Adoption Services, Denton, TX.

Ajakai Jaya (Chevalier), PhD, Licensed Professional Counselor and Family Therapist, Indian Counseling Agency, Buffalo, WY.

Robin Jennings, BS, Human Resource Manager, Simmons Mattress Co., Dallas, TX.

Sharon Jennings, MS, Librarian, Woodrow Wilson School, Denton, TX; craftswoman and owner of Mousekins Nook.

John Johansen, PhD, Clinical Psychologist for Adolescent Forensic Program at Vernon State Hospital, Vernon, TX.

Charles F. Kemp, PhD (deceased), formerly Professor of Pastoral Care and Psychology, Brite Divinity School, Texas Christian University.

Willa Lister, MS, Counselor, Fort Worth, TX.

Vicki McCall, MS, Elementary School Counselor, Arlington, TX.

Paul McDaniel, MS, Counselor at Jesuit College Preparatory High School, Dallas, TX.

Laura McLachlin, PhD, Associate Professor of Recreation and Park Management, University of California at Chico.

Jerre Miller, MS, Counselor, Fort Worth, TX.

Sherrie Moore, BS, Pharmaceutical Sales, Fort Worth, TX.

Nola Payne, MEd, Counselor, Fort Worth, TX.

David A. Wright, MS, Director of Public Information, North Lakes College, Irving, TX.

Foreword

Activity is the only road to knowledge.

George Bernard Shaw

Throughout the life span, activities play an integral role in our growth and development. Not only do they serve as outlets for excess energy, activities are also important learning tools. As infants, we learn concepts and problem-solving skills through active exploration and interaction with the world around us. Later, we experiment with games and exercises which enhance physical and cognitive skills. As adults, we continue to seek out activities which provide opportunities to master the environment.

Human beings are innately driven to function adaptively and effectively in a multitude of environments and within many interpersonal relationships. Activities and exercises such as those contained in this volume offer a supportive backdrop against which to practice adaptation, and to learn to distinguish function and dysfunction.

Active participation in these exercises allows participants to explore and practice healthy behaviors with guidance and support. It gives them an opportunity to examine their own feelings, to become aware of the perceptions of others, to explore and alter their patterns of communication, and to reflect on aspects of their lives which they may wish to change. Drs. Jennings and McManus have assembled an exceptional collection of exercises designed for a variety of populations and situations. These activities are as creative in nature as the audiences for whom they are designed and the individuals who will benefit from them. They are designed to be used by marriage and family therapists, counselors, family life educators, parent educators, occupational therapists, teachers, social workers, human resource personnel, management, and any number of educational, health, or business professionals who are in positions to work with other individuals and groups.

The format of the book lends itself to easy and efficient use. The exercises are organized into categories and a brief description of each category is provided for review. Each activity is then formatted so that the user can immediately determine whether it is appropriate for the needs of the group in terms of purpose, materials, and time available.

This first volume of *Structured Exercises for Promoting Family and Group Strengths* is an exciting and unique compilation of activities designed to promote growth in cognitive and affective domains. These exercises will provide a springboard for positive growth and development in individuals and groups. We are grateful for this first creative collection and look forward to future volumes.

Judith Carson Vestal, MA, LOTR
Assistant Professor
Louisiana State University at Shreveport

Preface

Structured Exercises for Promoting Family and Group Strengths is a resource providing experiential materials for training, education, and counseling. All the material provides an experiential approach that actively involves the participant–as a whole person–in the learning process.

This handbook will be of value to trainers, consultants, social workers, probation and correctional workers, counselors, teachers, pastors, chaplains, adult educators, nurses, managers, group workers, health educators, psychologists, family therapists, and physicians. The handbook offers a catalyst for dramatic change in people's lives.

This volume of *Structured Exercises for Promoting Family and Group Strengths* contains 71 new structured exercises, complete with step-by-step instructions for easy use. Some utilize new applications of familiar group processes and techniques. Others were submitted by people like you who continually strive to add the creative touch in their work. All have been field-tested with a variety of audiences.

Please note our policy for reproduction of the handbook contents. Our purpose in publishing these volumes is to foster interprofessional networking and to provide a framework through which we can all share our most effective ideas with each other. The layout is designed for easy photocopying of worksheets and training notes.

Feel free to adapt and duplicate any sections of the handbook for your use in training or educational events–as long as you use the proper citation as indicated on the copyright page. However, all materials are still covered by copyright. Prior written permission from The Haworth Press, Inc. is required if you plan large-scale reproduction or distribution of any portion of the handbook. If you wish to include any material in another publication for sale, please send us your request and proposal.

In the handbook series, we have shared our best with you and hope you will return the favor. We encourage you to submit your favorite structured exercises for inclusion in future volumes. You will find instructions in the Future Contributors section at the back of the book. Let us know what works well for you so that we can carry on the tradition of providing a forum for the exchange of innovative teaching designs.

A special note for using this volume is that we strongly urge trainers to view the group as a family and the family as a group. Throughout this volume, the terms "group" and "family" are used interchangeably, and the trainer should view the dynamics of both in much the same way. What works for a group will work with a family. We believe that wherever individuals go in life, they continually put effort into trying to recreate and solve issues around their families of origin. Yes, we believe that most people spend much effort at their work sites attempting to recreate the families they grew up in. Thus, as we explore group work, we learn about each others' families.

Introduction

Over the past three decades, there has been an emphasis on social skills in psychotherapy, training, and education. Clients have been taught to be open, candid, honest, and self-revealing. These social skills have been an area of interest and research for several decades. The works of Wolpe (1958), Ziegler and Phillips (1961), and Lazarus (1971) offered insight concerning the need for social skills training. The study by Frank (1974) showed how social skills training was one of the most positive outcomes in brief therapy. Social skills training is most beneficial as an intentional endeavor.

Welford (1980) pointed out that what is often called "skill" results in the efficient and effective use of strategies. The works of Trower, Bryant, and Argyle (1978) and Argyle (1975) studied techniques and areas of clinical application of social skills. L'Abate and Milan (1985, p. 6) suggested that "social skill is proactive, prosocial, and reciprocally productive of mutually shared reinforcement." Social skills learned and practiced in one context may be transferred to other contexts. Many studies have suggested that the lack of social skills often is associated with social disorganization (Phillips, 1968; Dohrenwend and Dohrenwend, 1969; and Phillips, 1978). Social disorganization is the lack of social competence in one's general state of affairs. The individual lacks the skills to meet the situation. The use of structured exercises is a strategy for exploring and teaching skills.

Over the past three decades there has been a tremendous growth and interest in marital and family therapy. Gurin, Veroff, and Feld (1960) reported on the basis of a nationwide survey that marital difficulties were the most frequently cited reason for consulting a mental health professional. Mental health statistics indicate that marital difficulties are among the three most common reasons that individuals seek the help of mental health professionals (Prochaska and Prochaska, 1978). Many relationship difficulties center around the lack of social skills (e.g., assertiveness, honesty, feelings and expressing feelings, candidness, open communication, etc.). This handbook presents an array of techniques for teaching and reinforcing social skills for successful relationships.

This handbook has been written with two purposes in mind: first, to offer practical "how to" information about techniques for assessing relationships; and second, to suggest methods and techniques for intervening in and enhancing relationships whether within a dyad, family, or group. It is hoped that the format of this handbook will make the materials readily useable and easily adaptable.

Each of the six sections in this handbook addresses therapeutic needs, and offers ways to deal with limitations that occur in couple, family, and group relationships and interpersonal behaviors. Social skills are taught and intervention techniques are offered.

REFERENCES

Argyle, M. (1975). *Bodily communication.* London: Methuen.

Dohrenwend, B. R. and Dohrenwend, B. S. (1969). *Social status and psychological inquiry.* New York: Wiley.

Frank, J. (1974). "Therapeutic components of psychotherapy: A 25 year progress report of research." *Journal of Nervous and Mental Disease, 159,* 325-342.

Gurin, G., Veroff, J. and Feld, S. (1960). *Americans view their mental health: Joint Commission on Mental Health.* Monograph series no. 4. New York: Basic Books.

L'Abate, L. and Milan, M. (1985). *Handbook of social skills training and research.* New York: Wiley.

Lazarus, A. (1971). *Behavior therapy and beyond.* New York: McGraw-Hill.

Phillips, L. (1968). *Human adaptation.* New York: Academic Press.

Phillips, L. (1978). *The social skills basis of psychopathology: Alternative to abnormal psychology and psychiatry.* New York: Grune & Stratton.

Prochaska, J. and Prochaska, J. (1978). "Twentieth-century trends in marriage and marital therapy." In T. Paulino and B. McCrady (Eds.), *Marriage and marital therapy: Psychoanalytic, behavioral and systems theory perspectives.* New York: Brunner/Mazel.

Trower, P., Bryant, B., and Argyle, M. (Eds.) (1978). *Social skills and mental health.* London: Methuen.

Welford, A. (1980). "The concept of skill and its application to social performance." In W. Singleton, P. Spurgeon, and R. Stammers (Eds.), *The analysis of social skills.* London: Plenum.

Wolpe, J. (1958). *Psychotherapy by reciprocal inhibition.* Palo Alto: Stanford University Press.

Ziegler, E. and Phillips, L. (1961). "Social competence and outcome in psychiatric disorder." *Journal of Abnormal and Social Psychology, 63,* 264-271.

A Guide for Using This Handbook

Group dynamics are the interactions that occur between individuals. Group members need to understand not only the "why" of what they have chosen to do but also "how" their actions are understood by other participants.

Structured Exercises for Promoting Family and Group Strengths offers 71 exercises you can use to help individuals, dyads, groups, and families become happier in relationships. Each exercise is structured to creatively involve people in the learning process, whatever the setting and the constraints, whatever the sophistication level of the participants. All exercises are appropriate for workshop format. The exercises are also appropriate for use by the professional while working with clients, or the exercises can be utilized as homework assignments. To aid you in the selection of appropriate exercises, they are grouped into six sections of this handbook under the following broad categories:

- *Icebreakers:* These short, 10- to 20-minute, lively exercises are designed to introduce people to the subject of group dynamics and to each other in a workshop experience.
- *Assessors:* These processes are designed both to help people gain information about each other and to offer constructive direction for better communication patterns. By accurately assessing the current situation, individuals can gain insight and direction that will assist them in better dealing with related issues that may arise in the future. In this section you will find a mixture of shorter assessments and major theme developers. Any exercise can be contracted or expanded easily to fit your purpose.
- *Dyad/Couple Discussion Starters:* These exercises are designed to assist dyads who find themselves in dysfunctional situations, where the communication pattern, trust level, and

emotional bond need to be examined and better understood. The dynamics of the relationship often go unnoticed until conflicts begin to emerge. The exercises assist the dyad both in examining and in establishing effective communication patterns. This occurs by offering specific areas for discussion such as roles, actions, and values and sexuality.

- *Group/Family Discussion Starters:* These exercises are designed to be used by the entire group or family. Examination of how the group functions, or dysfunctions, involves examining numerous patterns of living. These exercises assist the members in reflecting on many issues that affect their lives. The issues which are examined all pertain to areas of relationships that all individuals should be able to understand and participate in, no matter their age or sophistication level.
- *Enhancers:* This category of exercises provides undertakings that create a sense of self-esteem and self-fulfillment for the individual. The exercises create an environment of self-exploration. Participants draw together their insights and determine actions they wish to take on their own behalfs.
- *Energizers:* The eight energizers are intended to perk up the group whenever fatigue sets in. Sprinkle them throughout your program to illustrate skills or concepts. Try one for a change of pace–everyone's juices (including yours) will be flowing again in five to ten minutes.

The handbook format is designed for easy use. You will find that each exercise is described completely, including:

- Brief Description
- Objectives
- Materials Needed
- Group Composition
- Time Required
- Rationale
- Procedures
- Variations
- Trainer's Notes

The instructions are written primarily for large group workshop settings (30-100 people). However, most of the exercises work just as well with small groups, and, with little modification, they also can be quite useful in working with families and individuals or for personal reflection.

If you are teaching in a workshop or large group setting, we believe that the use of small discussion groups is the most potent learning structure available to you. We have found that groups with four persons each provide ample "air time" and a good variety of interaction.

These personal "sharing groups" allow people to make positive contact with each other and encourage them to personalize their experiences in depth. On evaluations, some people will say "Drop this," others will say "Give us more small group time," but most will report that the time you give them to share with each other becomes the heart of the workshop.

If you are working with an intact group of 12 people or less, you may at times want to keep the whole group together for process and discussion time rather than divide into the suggested four- or six-person groups. Let groups meet together two, three, or more times before forming new groups.

Each trainer has personal strengths, biases, pet concepts, and processes. We expect and encourage you to expand and modify what you find here to accommodate your style. Adjust the exercises as you see fit. Bring these designs to life for your participants by inserting your own content and examples into your teaching. Experiment!

And when you come up with something new, let us know. . . .

SECTION ONE:
ICEBREAKERS

CHAPTER SUMMARIES

Chapter 1.   **How Perceptive Are You?**

An eye-opening exercise to help people see how much attention they pay to details, and how events can be viewed differently. Each participant is given the same picture to examine closely, then asked questions about what was perceived.

Chapter 2.   **My Famous Person**

An exercise for helping the group/family to get to know each other better as each participant gives the group/family five hints to the identity of a famous person that he or she respects.

Chapter 3.   **A Positive Beginning**

This exercise is designed to help group members become better acquainted while building group or agency morale. It fosters solidarity by encouraging individuals to focus on and express personal and group strengths.

Chapter 4.   **The Beauty of Others**

This exercise can be used with a family or group to communicate appreciation of each other. Each member is asked to identify a flower that is symbolic of each other member. The beauty of the flower should represent the beauty of the target person.

Chapter 5.   Getting to the Root!

Group members become acquainted by learning about each others' roots. This exercise helps to develop understanding toward others and facilitates working conditions and intimacy by requiring participants to engage each other with specific questions about family conditions and histories.

Chapter 6.   Initial Feelings

This exercise helps group members recognize their feelings of discomfort and the coping behaviors they use when faced with new environments. Increased awareness of these feelings and actions enables participants to better understand themselves and others.

Chapter 7.   Are You More Like . . .

Participants become acquainted with each other without having to express themselves verbally. Through the use of semantic differential extremes, participants are challenged to reveal more of who they are. They must decide which extreme they are more like, then congregate with others who share the same identity.

Chapter 8.   Introductions Through Movements

This nonverbal exercise adds a new dimension to getting to know others in a short time period. It spices up introductions and brings many surprises to the group.

Chapter 9.   What I Did Well

This exercise focuses attention on the positive aspects of life. Through the sharing of problems and how they were solved, everyone has the opportunity to see the best in each other. This provides a basis for developing personal strengths and an attitude of

"*I can.*" It also develops a sense of comradery, and sets a positive tone for the rest of the day.

Chapter 10. Mirroring Yourself to Others

By revealing our values and showing our strengths we learn more about each other. Reflecting our choices tells others much about ourselves.

Chapter 11. Cheers!

By taking on the roles of characters from the popular television show, *Cheers*, participants have the opportunity to reveal traits they value, admire, or dislike in themselves or in others.

Chapter 12. Life Crest

This exercise provides an opportunity for a group or family to share with each other the things each holds dear. Each person completes a Life Crest with pictures or symbols, then explains the significance of the illustrations.

How Perceptive Are You?

Ron McManus

Brief Description: An eye-opening exercise to help people see how much attention they pay to details, and how events can be viewed differently. Each participant is given the same picture to examine closely, then asked questions about what was perceived.

Objectives:
1. To show individuals how perception can affect thoughts.
2. To accent the variety of interpretations available as different individuals perceive the same picture.
3. To focus the group's attention on the dynamics of group and family interactions.

Materials Needed: An appropriate picture, one copy for each person in the group. Any picture can be used; the more the picture fits the background of the participants, the more successful the experience. As an example, an illustration titled *The Family in Focus* is included and used for this exercise.

Group Composition: Any size group from very small (two or more) to extremely large. The larger the group, the more varied the perceptions; the more varied the ages and backgrounds of the members, the more diverse the perceptions and interpretations.

Time Required: Ten to 20 minutes, depending upon the size of the group, and the picture presented.

Rationale: Many things go unnoticed or appear unimportant to us at first glance. An analogy can be made between how we miss the details of the picture and how we overlook the details of a relationship.

Procedures:
1. The trainer begins the exercise by highlighting the following points:

   - No two people view the same experience the same way, or remember the same key elements.
   - Perception is the mind's interpretation of what is seen; people often see things differently.
   - People often see and hear what they expect to see and hear.
   - The following activity is to help individuals see how their interactions with others can be affected by their perceptions.

2. The trainer introduces the exercise by distributing copies of the picture, *The Family in Focus.*
3. Next tell everyone to examine the picture closely for five minutes and that at the end of that time they will be asked questions about it.
4. After five minutes ask everyone to turn the picture over.
5. Select the most appropriate questions from The Trainer's Perception Guide to explore with the group.
6. Share some of the questions and encourage members to respond.
7. Now ask members to identify strengths they observed in the group's ability to perceive.
8. Ask the members to share what they learned about themselves and their perceptive abilities.
9. If the following points do not emerge, the trainer may want to highlight them:

   - It is amazing how some remember the details and how some remember the overall feelings.
   - Even in relationships, family members have their own views of every situation and remember a wide variety of different details.
   - Relationships can falter when attention to details is ignored.
   - In this gathering we examined the difference in viewpoints, saw how different viewpoints can affect our thoughts and feelings, considered how perceptions can affect relationships, and hopefully created a new shared memory.

10. Send the group away with their pictures and copies of the original answer sheet. This will give them the opportunity to use the exercise again.

Variations: Divide into small groups (five to ten members for each group). Have each group examine the picture closely for five minutes. Then ask the participants to write down as many relationship topics as they can recall that are dealt with in the picture. The group would then discuss the topics that are mentioned.

Here are some of the topics that are depicted in the example illustration: single lifestyle, sibling rivalry, family togetherness, swinging singles, family violence, traditional "at-home" mother, tract housing, child custody, child loneliness, child care, single-parent mother, loneliness of the elderly, men and women adopting same work roles, the law, the socially abandoned, apartment living, and divorce.

Trainer's Notes: The trainer should adjust the detail asked for to accommodate the perceptive skills of the participants, i.e., do not make it so difficult that participants are irritated and turned off. Also the trainer may want to substitute a picture which compliments the participants' shared work site.

THE TRAINER'S PERCEPTION GUIDE

1. How many on bicycles? (3)
2. A 2-door or 4-door convertible? (2-door)
3. What direction are T.V. antennas pointing? (2 left & 2 right)
4. How many entrances to school? (2)
5. How many joggers? Male or female? (1 male & 1 female)
6. Which house has T.V. satellite dish? (second from right)
7. What is different about window in house second from left? (people visible and only 1 pane)
8. The elderly lady has something in each hand; what? (cane and purse)
9. How many swing seats are there? (3)
10. How many children holding hands by day care sign? (4)
11. On one porch, a person is sitting. What is worn? (cap)
12. How many windowpanes are shown at day care center? (26)
13. How many baby carriages? (2)
14. How many trees? (1)
15. Does church have cross on steeple? (no)
16. How many flags? (2)
17. What animal is shown? (a cat)
18. How many pillars? (6)
19. How many steps for building with pillars? (4)
20. How many apartment doors are shown by elderly lady? (8)
21. How many people (all total)? (41)
22. Are both flags waving in same direction? (no)

Artwork courtesy of David A. Wright from his poster "The Family in Focus" announcing the lecture series held at North Lake College of Dallas County Community College District during 1986-1987.

My Famous Person

Robin Jennings

Brief Description: An exercise for helping the group/family to get to know each other better as each participant gives the group/family five hints to the identity of a famous person that he or she respects.

Objectives:
1. To break the ice if the group is made up of strangers.
2. To help group/family members know each other better.
3. To strengthen members' characters as they identify with a famous person.

Materials Needed: None.

Group Composition: Any number of group or family members. If the group is very large, it may be beneficial to divide into subgroups.

Time Required: Fifteen to 30 minutes for groups/families of four to eight members, and then about two minutes for each additional participant.

Rationale: Too often when groups of strangers come together for a workshop or seminar, the introductions are simple and reveal little about the members. This exercise has participants reveal a little about themselves by the famous persons they select to share with the group/family. If the group is a family, then the sharing of someone respected gives hints to the member's character and values. Thus group/family members will know each other better and should be able to communicate more easily.

Procedures:
  1. The trainer introduces the exercise by giving five hints about a famous person he or she respects.
  2. After five people try to guess the identity of the famous person, the trainer tells the name of the famous person and tells how he or she became interested in the person.
  3. Next the trainer tells the participants to think of someone famous they respect and to think of five hints about the famous person to share with the group/family.
  4. Then a volunteer begins the exercise by giving his or her name and five hints about the famous person. Then five volunteers try to guess who the famous person is. If someone guesses the famous person, the volunteer tells how he or she became interested in the famous person. If no one guesses the famous person, the volunteer tells the group who it is and how he or she became interested in the person. Participation moves to the next volunteer until everyone has had an opportunity to introduce himself or herself and his or her famous person.

Variations: Variation can be added to this exercise by having each participant act out a characteristic of the famous person. This can help strangers get beyond some of their intimidations. With family members, the acting out of a characteristic adds some humor. With some groups, a restriction that the famous person be connected to the group's identity can add a nice dimension to the exercise, e.g., salespeople–J.C. Penney; teachers–Horace Mann; nurses–Florence Nightengale, etc.

Trainer's Notes: This is simply an interesting way to have members introduce themselves and break the mundaneness of typical introductions.

A Positive Beginning

John Johansen

Brief Description: This exercise is designed to help group members become better acquainted while building group or agency morale. It fosters solidarity by encouraging individuals to focus on and express personal and group strengths.

Objectives:
1. To use positive characteristics of individuals and the group/agency to become acquainted.
2. To help all members to focus on the strengths of the group/agency.
3. To promote a sense of community, both individual to individual and individual to group/agency.
4. To set a positive tone for all activities that follow during the conference or workshop.

Materials Needed: None. However, the activity can be enhanced by providing name tags on which the participants list the positive characteristics of themselves or of their agency. This often results in participants putting more effort into getting close enough to look at each others' name tags and discussing the positives identified.

Group Composition: This activity can accommodate a group or family of any number, depending upon the time available. If the group is large, it may be more practical to split into subgroups of four to seven members each.

Time Required: For a group of six to ten members, the time requirement is usually about ten to 12 minutes. As the group increases in number, the time tends to increase to about 15 to 30 minutes.

Rationale: By asking individuals to focus on themselves and their strengths, a feeling of personal involvement and contribution to the workshop is established early on. Also by asking each person to identify strengths of the agency or family, a sense of positive community is established. This allows all participants to feel that they are important both as individuals and as members of the institution, agency, group, or family.

Procedures:
1. The leader asks the participants to take a few minutes to think about their personal strengths and the strengths of the agency/family.
2. The members are then asked to introduce themselves and give a personal strength they think they possess.
3. Next, members identify a strength they believe the group/agency possesses. This procedure is followed until each member in the group has had an opportunity to participate.

Variations: Instead of introducing themselves, members could introduce others and mention what the others have told them in terms of personal strengths and strengths of the group.

This exercise can be quite impressive when a recorder for the group writes the various strengths identified on a chalkboard or easel. This could result in a permanent record of the beautiful qualities of the individuals and group. The list could be displayed in a prominent place as motivation toward a "self-fulfilling prophecy," creating a continued sense of appreciation for each other.

Another variation of this exercise is to talk over "What I contribute to this agency/family" and "What the agency/family contributes to me." This promotes group identity and connectedness. This also could be made more meaningful by writing the responses on a chalkboard or easel for later display.

Trainer's Notes: The trainer should give special attention to building on the positive aspects of the exercise. Be wary of any attempts to sabotage the positive group-building. Do not tolerate any attempts to turn it into a gripe session. Keep it 100 percent positive by saying, "The other side of the story is *not* relevant here at this time!"

The Beauty of Others

Glen Jennings

Brief Description: This exercise can be used with a family or group to communicate appreciation of each other. Each member is asked to identify a flower that is symbolic of each other member. The beauty of the flower should represent the beauty of the target person.

Objectives:
1. To get to know each other better.
2. To build positive relationships among group members.
3. To promote a sense of appreciation for each other.
4. To share a sense of value for each member.

Materials Needed: Fresh flowers or artificial flowers can be used to make this activity more meaningful. If unavailable, the participants can simply use their memories and imaginations to recall and describe flowers that are symbolic of each member.

Group Composition: Any composition is appropriate for this activity; the group can be family or nonfamily and of any number up to about 15 members. If the group is larger than 15, it should be organized into subgroups of six to 12 members.

Time Required: For a group/family of four to eight the time is normally 15 to 20 minutes and increases proportionately for additional members.

Rationale: Many people find it difficult to compliment or say positive things about others. This exercise provides a vehicle for overcoming this reluctance. The positive stroking tends to boost relationships and each person's self-esteem. The exercise also provides opportunities for participants to practice receiving compliments, something many people have difficulty doing.

Procedures:
1. The leader instructs members to form a rather close circle.
2. The leader asks for or selects a target person to sit in the middle of the circle.
3. Each member in the circle selects a flower or thinks of a flower which is symbolic of the target person.
4. Each person then tells how the flower is symbolic of the target person.
5. Stress the importance of sincerity and that *only positive comments are appropriate!*

Variations: Many variations are possible ranging from using colored pieces of paper, marbles, small pieces of cloth, etc., in place of flowers. Also, it is possible to simply form a circle and have participants say complimentary things about the target person.

This exercise can be more meaningful if the flower is handed to the target person at the time the complimentary comment is said by each member.

A unique variation of this exercise is to have group members make the flower out of paper and give it to the target person as a "gift of compliment." This would require having crepe paper, string, and wire for stems available. It would also require more time.

Trainer's Notes: It is crucial that all participants share only positive comments about the target person. This is best if only one, two, or three target people are honored at one time (per day). Ideally, for this exercise to be most powerful, a week or more should pass between targeting individuals.

It has been found to be quite useful to keep a box of 40 to 60 artificial flowers available for leading group activities. These have been valuable in leading groups whether doing family enrichment, sexuality groups, parent education, college teaching, conducting workshops for nurses on "Philosophy to Theory to Practices," or marriage counseling. The value and applicability of the exercise is limited only by the creativity of the trainer.

Getting to the Root!

Glen Jennings

Brief Description: Group members become acquainted by learning about each others' roots. This exercise helps to develop understanding toward others and facilitates working conditions and intimacy by requiring participants to engage each other with specific questions about family conditions and histories.

Objectives:
1. To provide a vehicle for people to get to know each other in terms of their family conditions and histories.
2. To provide a mixer so that individuals introduce themselves to others rather than connecting to one person and isolating themselves.
3. To begin the communication processes for the group.

Materials Needed: Each participant will need a copy of the Roots Guide and a pencil. Name tags would be helpful but are not necessary.

Group Composition: The group can be of any number ranging from six to 100.

Time Required: The time required ranges from five to 15 minutes depending upon the time limit set by the trainer. With larger groups (over 25), the trainer may want to extend the time limit or create subgroups.

Rationale: Many times when strangers or even acquaintances come together, they tend to congregate into dyads or triads rather than circulating and getting to know more people. This exercise structures time and requires members to move about and introduce themselves to a larger number of people. One of the best ways to break the ice with strangers is to engage them in a brief conversation about their families. Since each person is a product of his or her family, this is also a way to quickly develop an understanding of others.

Procedures:
1. The trainer should introduce himself or herself to the group and share a few brief comments about his or her roots, e.g., birthplace, birth order, origin of given name, family member most like, grandfather's occupation, maternal ethnicity, etc.
2. Give all members a copy of the Roots Guide and make sure everyone has a pen or pencil.
3. Allow a few minutes for the participants to become familiar with the Roots Guide.
4. Inform them of the time limit, and briefly explain the general procedure, emphasizing that no one is to sign anyone else's sheet more than once.
5. If appropriate, suggest that the person having the most signatures on his or her paper when time is called will receive a prize for getting to know the most people.
6. Field any questions about the exercise.
7. Remind participants of the time limit, then start the exercise by saying "Begin."
8. At the end of the time limit, say "Time's up," then determine who has the most signatures.

Variations: The trainer may want to add or delete questions from the Roots Guide as deemed appropriate for the nature of the group. The exercise is easily modified for use with extended family and appropriate for use at family reunions.

Trainer's Notes: The trainer may want to use the general idea but make major changes in the guide sheet to accommodate the occupational background of the participants. For instance if the participants were salespeople, the guide sheet could address aspects about sales or products.

ROOTS GUIDE

Instructions:

Find one person to sign on a line; no person's signature should appear more than once on this paper. After introducing yourself and asking the other person a specific question from this sheet, move on to another person and introduce yourself again. Continue this process to see how many signatures you can secure before the leader says "Time's up!"

1. Locate someone who is named after her mother_____
2. Someone who is the first born_____
3. Someone with the same three initials as yours_____
4. Blue eyes_____
5. Named after his grandfather_____
6. A middle child_____
7. An only child_____
8. A parent who was a teacher_____
9. Had a stepfather_____
10. The youngest in the family_____
11. Over 35 years of age when first married_____
12. Father was a businessman_____
13. Grew up on a farm_____
14. Lived part of his/her life with grandparents_____
15. Is shorter than his/her parent of the same sex_____
16. Of Irish ancestry_____
17. Was born west of the Mississippi river_____
18. Attended a private school_____
19. Grew up in a bilingual home_____
20. Father was a career military man_____
21. Of Scandinavian ancestry_____
22. Mother was over 5'7"_____
23. A twin_____
24. Has an older sister_____
25. Born in a landlocked state_____
26. Has three or more sisters_____
27. Father was a minister_____
28. Grew up in a mountainous state_____

29. Born in a New England state_____
30. Followed in father's occupation_____
31. A Southerner by birth_____
32. Was born outside of the U.S._____
33. Has a fear of flying_____
34. Believes in reincarnation_____
35. Enjoys skiing (water or snow)_____
36. Born in the Northwest_____
37. Looks more like mother than father_____
38. Married out of his/her religion_____

Initial Feelings

Linda J. Brock

Brief Description: This exercise helps group members recognize their feelings of discomfort and the coping behaviors they use when faced with new environments. Increased awareness of these feelings and actions enables participants to better understand themselves and others.

Objectives:
1. To develop group members' abilities to observe their own uncomfortable feelings.
2. To help them become aware of the actions they take to restore comfort.

Materials Needed: Name tags.

Group Composition: Any group of people who are coming together for the first time.

Time Required: About ten to 15 minutes.

Rationale: People in new situations usually feel some discomfort and have developed somewhat automatic behaviors to make themselves more comfortable. People benefit from being able to recognize their negative feelings and become aware of their coping behaviors. By recognizing negative feelings people learn to modify their apprehensions in similar situations and become more sensitive to others' feelings.

Procedures:
1. Begin the exercise as soon as possible after everyone has entered and is seated in the room.
2. Ask the participants to think back a few minutes to when they first arrived and entered the room. What were they feeling? Assure them that any feelings are acceptable, the most typical being discomfort, anxiety, and nervousness.
3. Then ask them what they did first upon entering the room. Possibilities include: talking to someone, sitting next to someone they already knew, choosing a seat in the back near the door, leaving an empty seat between themselves and the next person, getting a drink of water, people-watching, reading workshop materials, etc. Discuss how such behaviors give people a sense of control and help ease discomfort.
4. Discuss how by becoming more aware of our own negative feelings and how we cope with them, we can better understand our family members, co-workers, customers, students, clients, etc.

Variations: With small groups it may be possible for members to share some of their coping actions and discuss how effective they are. Care should be taken to make the exercise nonjudgmental.

A nice variation of the exercise is to ask participants to identify one word which best describes the feelings they had upon entering the room. Ask them to write the word on their name tags, which are to be worn for the duration of the session. This most likely will lead each participant to meet and have discussions with more members of the group.

Trainer's Notes: This type of exercise can be used in a variety of settings other than at the beginning of a training session. With modification, it can be used to help participants process their feelings whenever a change is brought to a work environment, a business process, a change in the law governing people served by a public institution, a new procedure, a new boss or supervisor, a merger of departments, etc.

It is important for the trainer to maintain an accepting and supportive attitude when participants are sharing their feelings and processing what these feelings meant in the particular situation. One of the best ways for the trainer to do this is by sharing and processing his or her own feelings and their meanings. If the group is somewhat reluctant to participate, the trainer can help them feel more comfortable by revealing some of the things he or she felt upon entering the room.

Are You More Like . . .

Laura McLachlin

Brief Description: Participants become acquainted with each other without having to express themselves verbally. Through the use of semantic differential extremes, participants are challenged to reveal more of who they are. They must decide which extreme they are more like, then congregate with others who share the same identity.

Objectives:
1. To acquaint participants with one another.
2. To be able to recognize nonverbal expression.

Materials Needed: None.

Group Composition: Any size family (nuclear or extended) or group (known to each other or strangers).

Time Required: Ten to 25 minutes.

Rationale: Members may feel uncomfortable expressing themselves verbally to each other. This activity provides an opportunity for participants to express themselves nonverbally.

Procedures:
1. Instruct all participants to come to the center of the room (clear all chairs, tables, etc.).
2. Explain to the participants that you are going to call out pairs of words. They are to move to the left side of the room if they are more like the first word and to the right side of the room if

they are more like the second word. (Example: Are you more like a hiking boot or a ballet slipper? Hiking boots move to the left and ballet slippers move to the right.)

3. As each pair of words is called out, participants are to move to the side of their choice.
4. Encourage participants to notice who is in each group they choose to join. These individuals may share common interests or feelings.
5. Provide opportunities for individuals to share their perceptions and self-discoveries.

Variations: Any number of word pairs may be used. Word groups could be developed in which a common theme runs throughout the list of pairs, e.g., all foods, all animals, titles of books or songs, states, weather conditions, etc. For groups from business or industry, the word pairs could be specific to the work environment.

Trainer's Notes: This exercise works well with people who know each other or with total strangers. If participants are uncomfortable at first, the trainer could begin the exercise by sharing his or her own feelings and the meanings of them. Even if individuals do not identify strongly with either choice, encourage them to make a choice.

ARE YOU MORE LIKE . . .

1. Hiking Boots	Ballet Slippers
2. A Waltz	Break Dancing
3. A Cartoon	A Soap Opera
4. Mexican Food	French Food
5. A Novel	A Play
6. Planned	Spontaneous
7. A Quiet Evening	A Large Party
8. A State Park	A Resort
9. A Three-Piece Suit	Blue Jeans
10. A Motorcycle	A Luxury Car
11. A Dandelion	A Carnation
12. A Fax Letter	A Postcard
13. A Sun Worshiper	Nanook of the North
14. A Parent	A Child
15. Charlie Brown	Lucy
16. Cross-Country Skiing	Racquetball
17. A Mountain	A Valley
18. Morning	Evening
19. An Orange	An Apple

Introductions Through Movements

Laura McLachlin

Brief Description: This nonverbal exercise adds a new dimension to getting to know others in a short time period. It spices up introductions and brings many surprises to the group.

Objectives:
1. To provide a nonverbal format for introductions.
2. To increase self-awareness.
3. To increase assertiveness skills.
4. To become more expressive and more comfortable in expressing oneself.

Materials Needed: A copy of the Introduction Through Movements instruction sheet for each participant.

Group Composition: Small group or family.

Time Required: Fifteen to 45 minutes.

Rationale: Alternative methods of expression are important for individuals to assert themselves. By expressing themselves to each other, better awareness and understanding can develop among the group or family members.

Procedures:
1. Talk briefly about the awkwardness of introductions and of expressing oneself. Point out some of the ways we express ourselves through our movements, e.g., sadness, joy, tiredness, cold, disgust, etc.

2. Tell the participants that this exercise provides an opportunity to express themselves nonverbally. Each participant will choose a number and then express the word or phrase which goes with the number.
3. Instruct participants not to look at the Introduction Through Movements sheet while the expressor is going through a movement.
4. The participant expresses the movement number he/she has chosen. He/she will have one minute to express the movement chosen. The other participants will try to guess the feeling or mood expressed. After one minute of guessing the expressor will tell what he/she was trying to express and then tell the group his/her name.

Variations: Have participants make up their own movement statements and let others guess what mood or feeling they are trying to portray.

Trainer's Notes: A variety of music may be played during this exercise. If participants are feeling uncomfortable, the trainer should initiate the exercise by demonstrating movements to some of the attached movement/feeling statements.

INTRODUCTIONS THROUGH MOVEMENTS

Introduce yourself by expressing the movements for the number you have chosen. You should express the movement for one minute. Although someone may call out the movement, continue for the full minute. Afterwards introduce yourself to the group.

How would you walk or move when:

1. You are joyful.

2. You feel proud of something you have done.

3. You have lost a game.

4. You feel overwhelmed.

5. You feel powerless.

6. You think you have made a mistake.

7. You are embarrassed.

8. You are late to work.

9. You have won a lottery.

10. You feel boxed in.

11. You feel relieved after a crisis.

12. You feel free.

13. You have no concern with time.

14. You are worry free.

15. You are hurried.

16. You are emotionally hurt.

What I Did Well

Ajakai Jaya

Brief Description: This exercise focuses attention on the positive aspects of life. Through the sharing of problems and how they were solved, everyone has the opportunity to see the best in each other. This provides a basis for developing personal strengths and an attitude of "I *can.*" It also develops a sense of comradery, and sets a positive tone for the rest of the day.

Objectives:
1. To foster a sense of accomplishment for each participant.
2. To increase a sense of appreciation for self and others.
3. To help all see themselves as positive forces.

Materials Needed: None.

Group Composition: A family or group of four to eight members. Divide large groups into four- to-eight-member subgroups.

Time Required: Twenty to 40 minutes, depending upon the number of members in the group/subgroups.

Rationale: Too often we fail to focus on our strengths and accomplishments. By sharing with the group a difficult time or experience, everyone can become more in touch with his or her inner strengths and abilities. Focusing on difficulties and how each overcame them enables the group to look at pain as a part of the human condition. Participants will most likely develop greater appreciation and caring for each other as they share their experiences.

Procedures:
1. Participants are asked to think of a particular problem, difficulty, or challenge that they have experienced, and what they did to work through it.
2. The leader might share some personal challenge which he or she has experienced and overcome to become a better, stronger person. Examples might be the loss of a loved one or pet, an accident, a failure, a disappointment, a rejection, or a tragedy.
3. Allow each member to volunteer in turn to share his or her problem.

Variations: Some groups might benefit by having telegraphic sentences written on a chalkboard or easel as each member shares his or her story. These comments might be saved and posted someplace as a reminder, and for all to reflect on in the future.

Trainer's Notes: Often this exercise is enhanced by sitting rather closely together (especially by sitting on the floor if the group is comfortable doing so), and by the leader sharing a personal difficulty that he or she has had to work through. The leader should encourage sharing, listening, and the giving of compliments. Sometimes a very negative person may want to turn the exercise into a gripe or complaint session, and the leader should be prepared to redirect the focus if this happens. Be sure to close with some powerful statements about the many strengths that the different members have, and about how pain is a common part of life. The leader may find it helpful to briefly point out that humans often move to a higher state of life by working through their pain, challenges, and the existential aspects of life.

Mirroring Yourself to Others

Laura McLachlin

Brief Description: This is an exercise in self-exploration and self-revelation. Individual values, freedom of choice, getting in touch with one's strengths, and personal free time are some of the issues addressed.

Objectives:
1. To identify those activities that may enhance personal growth, well-being, and happiness.
2. To share one's values within small group interactions.

Materials Needed: Questionnaire, 5×8 index cards for making personalized name tags, pens or pencils, and chalkboard.

Group Composition: Family (nuclear or extended) group or small- to medium-sized group (five to 30 members). Larger groups may be subdivided into groups of five to seven members.

Time Required: Thirty to 90 minutes, depending upon the size of the group.

Rationale: Individuals often are not aware of how their values and choices affect their own lives and other people's lives. This exercise is rich in potential for exploration of personal values and choices, and for positive affirmation from group members. There are many possibilities for using this exercise and variations of it as an icebreaker.

Procedures:
1. See Trainer's Notes for beginning discussion.

41

2. Discuss the goals of the session. Distribute blank 5×8 index cards and pencils to all participants.

3. On the chalkboard, put the numerical layout of the name tag (see Questionnaire).

4. Have the group members answer the ten questions on their name tags (see Questionnaire).

5. Participants should form small groups (four to seven members). It will be a more meaningful experience if they get in a group with people they do not know well.

6. Participants should share their name tags. Explain that each participant will be given only three minutes to share any, all, or none of his/her name tag with the other people in the group. The other people cannot respond verbally. Call time at the end of each three minute period.

7. Once all group participants have had a chance to share their name tags, give the groups approximately ten minutes to respond to one another verbally. Suggest that the group members begin their feedback with "I liked it when you said. . . ."

8. Discussion may cover the following questions:

    a. Did you learn anything new about yourselves that you had not known before?

    b. Do you see any connection between your answers to these questions and your values?

    c. Did you find that you had many possible responses and that it was difficult to choose just one?

    d. Were there some questions that you did not want to answer?

    e. Were there some answers that you did not want to share with the others in the group?

    f. During feedback, was it difficult to give a compliment and/or receive one? Why?

Variations: The trainer may want to change any of the questions to fit the particular needs of the group or family. The trainer may choose not to create subgroups, or not to conduct the full-group discussion.

For variation the trainer may choose to have participants share their name tag in pairs or with the total group. There are unlimited ways to vary the discussion and introductions.

Trainer's Notes: Introductory discussion may include: Freedom of choice, personal free time and leisure experiences, desired changes, strengths and affirmations, values, etc. When discussing the goals of the activity, sort out such issues as: how personal choices affect individuals; how choices are viewed by others; and how to identify and make changes

When discussing the goals of the activity, sort out *"what counts."* This process requires support from friends and family members. Becoming aware of personal values and priorities can lead to a better life.

Be sure to allow ample time after reading each question for participants to think about and write down their answers.

MIRRORING YOURSELF TO OTHERS QUESTIONNAIRE

2		4
3		5

Numerical layout

of name tag   10

                               1

                               10

6		8
7		9

1. Write your name in fairly large letters, but no larger than about an inch high.
2. What is the name of the place where you spent the three happiest days *in a row* of your life?
3. Where do you most often go when you want to be alone? Or, where is your special "thinking place"?
4. If by magic you could change anything about your leisure participation, what would you change?
5. Who is the person in your life who brings you the most happiness or joy? Or, who makes you smile almost every time you see him or her?
6. When you make decisions, in what order do you: *think, feel, act?* That is, do you act before you think or feel; feel before you act and think; etc.? Arrange them in the order that is most often true of the way you make decisions.
7. What is your favorite activity? Or, what is the activity you look most forward to doing?
8. If you follow through on what you are now planning for your life, what will you be doing six months from now?
9. What new activities would you like to engage in?
10. What are *two* things about yourself that you are most proud of? That is, what can you do well that makes you feel special? Write these answers in a circle around your name.

11

Cheers!

Paul McDaniel

Brief Description: By taking on the roles of characters from the popular television show, *Cheers*, participants have the opportunity to reveal traits they value, admire, or dislike in themselves or in others.

Objectives:
1. To provide a vehicle for introductions and for group members to enjoy each other.
2. To allow group members to express themselves through role playing.
3. To open a dialogue on traits admired and/or disliked in people.

Materials Needed: An index card for each *Cheers* character: name printed in large letters on one side, and Character Profile descriptions on the other.

Group Composition: Group, couples, or family; any number of members.

Time Required: Twenty to 45 minutes, depending upon the length of discussion that is permitted.

Rationale: The participants' choices of particular *Cheers* characters can be indications of how they perceive the traits and behaviors of themselves and others. This exercise is also an opportunity for participants to express strengths they possess as well as needs they may have.

Procedures:

1. The trainer begins by announcing that he or she has been contacted by the producer of *Cheers* and informed that members from the group will be selected to take the place of the characters on the show.
2. The nine Character Profile cards are displayed so that everyone can see the names of the characters.
3. Nine members at a time come to the front and each select the card of the character that he or she would most enjoy playing.
4. Each member in turn tells the group which character he or she has chosen and explains why the character was chosen.

Variations: The trainer could ask the participants what traits they most admire in the characters they have selected and which characteristics they do not admire. The trainer could ask them to pick the characters they would least like to play.

The trainer could ask questions of the different characters and have them respond in the way that they think the *Cheers* character would respond. Also ask participants how they think they are like their *Cheers* characters and how they think they are different. Give attention to the comfort level of the group in terms of self-disclosure.

The trainer could select two or three people from the group to interact in certain situations as the characters they have selected. Examples: Norm, Carla, and Frasier meeting on the first day of high school; Woody, Sam, and Cliff discussing what their ideas of perfect dates would be.

Allow the audience to interview each character. Suggest that they ask things they have thought they would like to ask the real *Cheers* characters.

Some groups may enhance this exercise by coming up with their own profiles for each character.

Trainer's Notes: Many people think that they could be someone else. This is an easy way to let people tell what they think of themselves or wish they could be. It could help determine who in the group is creative and open and wants to explore some personal changes.

If it appears that more than one person wants to select a particular character it may be necessary to suggest that not everyone could be the same character, especially Norm. Be creative in suggesting that this allows them to "try on" different characters and different behaviors.

To help the group to get into role playing, the trainer could have a variety of situations printed on index cards. The situations could be general, or specific to the group's work setting, family situation, or problem. General situations could be: deciding on a movie to view or a restaurant to eat at; who to invite to a party; etc. Specific situations could be: who gets the difficult jobs at work; how to confront a busybody at a job site; how promotions are determined; selecting the next role-playing situation; who and how one family member is to break bad news to a parent; etc.

CHARACTER PROFILES FOR CHEERS

Sam Malone–lives for today, childlike, immature, carefree, never thinks about anything serious, often self-centered, thinks he is a ladies' man.

Diane Chambers–goal-oriented, precise, articulate, likes to use big words, has high opinion of herself, well-educated, intelligent but has difficulty with relationships.

Rebecca Howe–takes life seriously, seems to be unable to find the relationship that is right for her, low self-esteem, beautiful, career-minded.

Cliff Claven–nerdish, knows more about subjects than others care to know about, lives with his mother, others cannot figure out why he has an inflated ego.

Carla Tortelli–mother of six, abrasive, opinionated, goes with her feelings, says whatever she wants, intimidates everyone, good sense of humor, has little regard for men and often thinks all men are pigs.

Woody Boyd–naive, innocent, total optimist, small-town ways, enjoys life, trusts all people, believes strongly in family values.

Norm Peterson–everyone's friend, sloppy, no career aspirations, lives for the moment, values male bonding, never puts up a front for anyone–what you see is what you get.

Frasier Crane–intelligent, artistic, cautious, misfit in this group but values their relationships, struggles with his desire to be a part of this group even though his intellect tells him it is valueless.

Lilith Sternin-Crane–career woman, intelligent, often uptight, serves as the group's conscience, calculating, cautious, when she lets loose everybody looks out.

Life Crest

Lee Hipple

Brief Description: This exercise provides an opportunity for a group or family to share with each other the things each holds dear. Each person completes a Life Crest with pictures or symbols, then explains the significance of the illustrations.

Objectives:
1. To have participants identify important characteristics about themselves.
2. To depict these characteristics through the medium of art to facilitate later discussions.
3. To help participants see one another in a new way.

Materials Needed: A copy of the Life Crest for each member; a variety of felt pens, crayons, or colored pencils for drawing.

Group Composition: Three to ten members, depending upon the time available. However, larger groups or multiple families could be divided into smaller groups. This exercise can be used effectively with anyone, from school-aged children through adults, with some variations in the questions asked.

Time Required: Thirty to 90 minutes, depending on group size. Allow about 20 minutes for drawing, and about three to six minutes for each person to explain his or her drawing.

Rationale: The use of symbols or pictures to depict important life events, values, and beliefs can help to conceptualize these things in a new way. As group members listen to explanations of each other's drawings, they may come to know each other in a different and perhaps closer way.

Procedures:
1. Talk briefly to the group about values (appreciating self and others'), and explain the purpose of Life Crests (their self-revealing benefits). Then explain that each member is going to have the chance to make his or her own Life Crest.
2. Distribute copies of the Life Crest and allow members to choose drawing utensils.
3. Explain that each participant is to use only symbols or pictures to respond to the questions asked for each section of the Life Crest.
4. Allow time for participants to complete their Life Crest.
5. Encourage participants to explain their Life Crests to the group.
6. Discuss some of the following issues: What did you learn about yourself from this exercise? What do you appreciate about another person's crest?

Variations: This exercise can be varied quite easily by using different questions. Questions can be developed about the past, present, or future, and concern topics such as: values, traits, events, dreams, fears, jobs, life scenes, beliefs, family characteristics, etc.

Members could use old magazines to cut out pictures to paste onto the Life Crest to make a collage to depict their answers to the questions. The exercise can become more metaphorically self-revealing by using more abstract materials, such as: objects from nature, leaves, shells, twigs, bark, etc.; tickets, or other nondescript pieces of colored paper, torn into various shapes; and so on.

Trainer's Notes: The trainer should be aware that some participants may feel uncomfortable or embarrassed because they do not believe themselves to be skilled artists. This problem can be avoided by assuring everyone that all drawings will be equally accepted. The exercise is both a learning and fun experience.

LIFE CREST QUESTIONNAIRE

The following are some questions which can be used for completing the Life Crest. The trainer can select from these questions or create others which are more specific for the group or family.

1. What has been your most meaningful achievement since you became an adult? (This could be changed to: since you started school, or became a teenager; or within the past month, year; etc.)
2. What was the happiest time for you during the past year?
3. What is something that you would not give up?
4. What symbolizes "heaven" for you?
5. "You will die in one year." What would you want to do in that year's time if you were guaranteed success?
6. Identify where you are now by a symbol or picture in terms of transition. (This could be changed to: Where do you want to be in a certain time in the future?)
7. Draw a tree which could be symbolic of your sense of trust in relationships.
8. Identify the book which you have most enjoyed. (This could be the book which has touched your life the most, the one you return to most often, your favorite, etc.)
9. Draw a picture which gives you a sense of peace.
10. Draw an animal to symbolize a value you hold dear.
11. Identify one of your favorite songs.
12. Draw a picture to express your sense of contentment.
13. Identify the characteristics you most admire in others.
14. What is one of your favorite quotes?
15. Draw a flower to represent your current internal state (emotion).

LIFE CREST

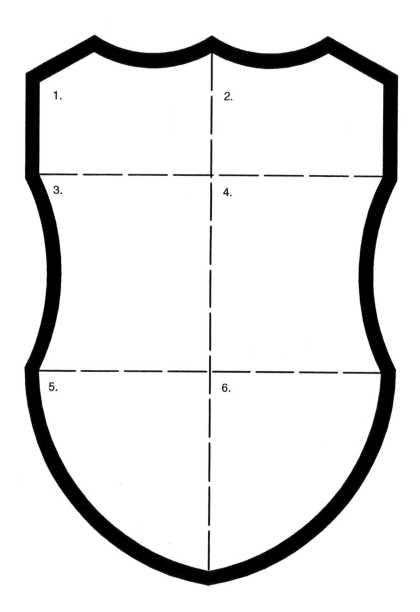

SECTION TWO:
ASSESSORS

CHAPTER SUMMARIES

Chapter 13.   **Fishbowl**

A group activity to sensitize teachers or others working with multicultures. The activity can be used as an in-service training activity.

Chapter 14.   **Charting Your Actions**

Each group/family member picks a circle tab(s) that represents each group member's actions or words during a set period (a day or a week).

Chapter 15.   **Relationship Value Profile**

Values are subtle foundations that guide the day-to-day activities of groups/families and their members. This exercise helps the group/family identify the things they want out of life. Group/family members rank the group/family's wants as they see them, as well as their own wants.

Chapter 16.   **Dyad Assessment: Accelerator and Brake**

This exercise can be used by the trainer or the couple to identify areas of the marriage that need adjustment. It can provide an index for determining the area and the amount of adjustment needed to develop a more satisfying relationship.

Chapter 17.   Dyadic Sexual Satisfaction Inventory

An exercise that can be used with couples to evaluate their level of sexual satisfaction and initiate communication about the sexual area of their relationship. There are 20 areas of sexual satisfaction which each member of the couple evaluates and an opportunity to make specific comments which can lead to sexual counseling and sexual enrichment.

Chapter 18.   Fighting Patterns

A simple checklist of common destructive fighting patterns which can serve as a worksheet for change.

Chapter 19.   What Is Important?

Identifying personal values is important to self-concept as well as to family/group identity. This exercise helps group members to identify personal values and to explore how they are different from and similar to others' values.

Chapter 20.   Taking Your Vital Signs

By identifying all the information we possess, we are better able to improve our communication with others. Sorting out feelings, thoughts, intentions, etc. helps improve understanding of self and improves communication.

Chapter 21.   Strikes, Spares, Splits, and Gutterballs

This exercise is based loosely on the game of bowling. Each participant takes a turn responding to a hypothetical question or problem, and the other players rate his or her response as either a strike, spare, split, or gutterball. This exercise fosters better communication, creativity in problem solving, and an expansion of options in relationships within a fun/game setting.

Chapter 22.   Let's Make a Picture

Improving decision-making skills fosters positive relationships and leads to greater productivity. Finding out who is a follower and who is a leader can be quite revealing when making a picture and solving a problem.

13

Fishbowl

Nola Payne
Jerre Miller
Willa Lister
Dixie Dibley
Ron McManus
Glen Jennings

Brief Description: A group activity to sensitize teachers or others working with multicultures. The activity can be used as an in-service training activity.

Objectives:
1. To promote understanding and awareness of cultural, generational, and age differences and similarities.
2. To promote group solidarity and a sense of caring.
3. To open avenues of communication for reducing tension between group/family members.

Materials Needed: For each participant: a set of Response Rating Cards. For each subgroup: two fishbowls, Situation Cards, and Role Stereotype Cards. For trainer's use: chalkboard or easel.

Group Composition: Any size group (as varied as possible in terms of ethnicity and age) or family, divided into four-, six-, or eight-member subgroups.

Time Required: About 45 to 60 minutes.

Rationale: Tensions often develop between different members of a group or family as a result of the different roles assigned to the members, or as a result of how members implement their respective roles. This exercise helps people to focus on this tension in a rather playful way, and to begin the processes of change and understanding. Adults and children need to examine how they perceive and relate to each other. Role-playing tends to magnify these processes and provides an opportunity to have fun while beginning to make changes.

Procedures:
1. Begin the exercise by dividing the participants into subgroups.
2. Appoint a facilitator for each group who will be responsible for keeping the group on task.
3. Distribute a set of Response Rating Cards to each participant.
4. Each facilitator appoints or asks for two volunteers within the group. One person will "act" as a member (adult, boss, clerk, co-worker, etc.) in a role play situation, and the other person will "act" as the opposing member (child, employee, buyer, co-worker, etc).
5. The trainer gives two fishbowls to each group.
6. Situation Cards are placed in one fishbowl and Role Stereotype Cards are placed in the other.
7. The adult role-player selects a Situation Card and the child role-player selects a Role Stereotype Card. The child assumes the role on the Role Stereotype Card, and the adult ssumes the role of discussing with the child the situation on the Situation Card. The object of the role-play exchange is to show how situations can be perceived differently by people.
8. After the role play, the other group members will respond to the effectiveness of the interchange by displaying a response rating card. Their ratings are based on how effectively a resolution was brought about in the role-play exchange. The cards are rated 1 to 5 (1 = least effective, 5 = most effective). Group members should provide comments and insight as they explain their response rating.
9. Assemble everyone back together and have the group respond to the Discussion Questions.

10. Conclude the session by writing on a chalkboard or easel the major conclusions drawn from the discussion questions.

Variations: The groups do not have to have a diversity of ages. Groups of like ages could easily role-play each other.

This exercise can be modified easily to allow supervisors and supervisees to role-play each other, and to begin the process of changing behaviors to promote better communication and greater productivity.

Also clerks and other employees can role-play the inappropriate behaviors of each other.

This exercise can be very effective with families by allowing them to see each other's behaviors. If the family members can role-play each other and see the humor in their interactions, they are likely to make some changes and become closer. This activity could most likely be very therapeutic as the parents see themselves through the eyes of the children, and the children see themselves through the eyes of the parents. There are likely to be real benefits in the husband seeing himself through the eyes of the wife or children, and like benefits in the wife seeing herself through the eyes of the husband or children. The trainer needs to be aware that some families may be so stressed that they cannot enter into this activity in the appropriate playful mood. Such families will need to be in counseling and work out some of their problems before they could benefit from this role-playing exercise.

Trainer's Notes: Since this exercise involves more detail than most others in this handbook, it is wise to do a few practice runs with acquaintances before undertaking it with large groups. Also, if the tension is too great between different members, they may have great difficulty getting into this activity. In this situation it behooves the trainer to spend some time talking about the difficulties, vulnerabilites, and challenges involved in looking at ourselves. At the same time, the trainer should point out the rewards of doing so, and mention that role-playing can be an appropriate and fun way to do this.

FISHBOWL CARDS

The trainer should prepare an adequate number of both types of cards. Three-by-five index cards are usually the easiest to use for making cards.

Situation Cards	Role Stereotype Cards
Late with homework	Father or Husband
Misbehaving in class	Mother or Wife
Tardy to school/class	Hispanic
Did not bring materials	African-American
Disruptive behavior	Preppie
Rude behavior by clerk to buyer	New Wave Rocker
Skipped class	Jock
Inappropriate display of affection	Cowboy
Parent shaming child	Poverty Child
Carelessly broken science equipment	Druggie

RESPONSE RATING CARDS

These can be made of three-by-five index cards by simply writing the numbers "1" through "5" on the cards. Prepare enough so that each participant receives a set of five cards.

DISCUSSION QUESTIONS

1. Which role was most difficult? Why?
2. What are some "role stereotype" similarities and differences of which you are now more aware?
3. What were your feelings when you received a lower response effectiveness rating than you felt you deserved?
4. How did this experience affect your feelings about communication across generations?
5. What, if anything, did you learn about cultural differences?
6. Why should we be more empathic with others and their behaviors?

14

Charting Your Actions

Ron McManus

Brief Description: Each group/family member picks a circle tab(s) that represents each group member's actions or words during a set period (a day or a week).

Objectives:
1. To examine the patterns of words and actions in relationships.
2. To see the contributions of each participant to the relationship.

Materials Needed: Family Chart, enlarged or redrawn to poster board size; stick-on tabs, made by trainer or purchased.

Group Composition: Small groups (two to eight members), or if group is larger divide into smaller groups.

Time Required: Determined by the group (usually 30 to 60 minutes).

Rationale: Relationships need feedback to understand how each person's words and actions are seen by the others.

Procedures:
1. Open the exercise with the following comments:
   - People are often not aware of how they are seen and understood by others.
   - Intimate relationships need a feedback of information concerning the individuals' actions.
   - This exercise is to help you chart how you observe other people's actions.

2. Divide the group into two- to eight-member subgroups.
3. Instruct each member to recall other family/group member's positive or negative actions or words that helped strengthen the relationship. After sharing this with the family/group, the individual places a tab on the appropriate track of the chart that will represent the identified feeling or emotion.
4. Bring closure to the exercise by asking participants to share with the larger group what the exercise has meant to them and their relationships.

Variations: This exercise can be modified to fit many groups who work as small units of two to eight members. There is much to be gained from using this exercise in the work setting–improved communication, a sense of caring and appreciation, and increased productivity.

Trainer's Notes: The stick-on tabs can be made by the trainer, but it is suggested that the type sold at office supply or variety stores be purchased. These are available in a variety of colors, which could be assigned to various emotions or feelings. For example: blue, a pleasant emotion; yellow, friendship or trust and other such feelings; red, volatile emotions or feelings such as anger, hate, envy, etc.; green, growth-related emotions and feelings; etc.

FAMILY CHART

STICK-ON TABS

(Blank tabs can be purchased, then simply write in appropriate words.)

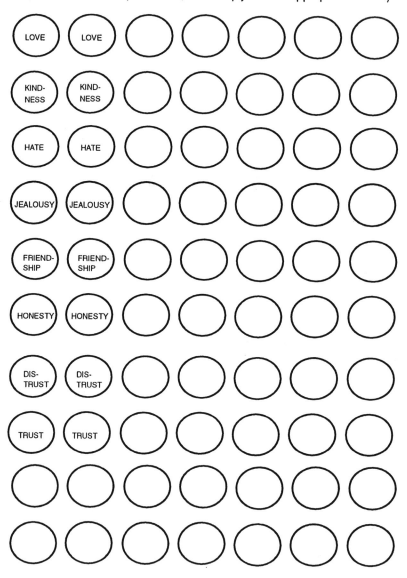

15

Relationship Value Profile

Glen Jennings

Brief Description: Values are subtle foundations that guide the day-to-day activities of groups/families and their members. This exercise helps the group/family to identify the things they want out of life. Group/family members rank the group/family's wants as they see them, as well as their own wants.

Objectives:
1. To provide a basis for initiating family examination of values and value differences.
2. To facilitate family communication in an area that often operates at a less than conscious level.
3. To promote family cohesiveness and equality as each family member has an opportunity to influence the family unit's values.

Materials Needed: Pens and copies of the Family Value Profile.

Group Composition: As many family members as possible, or any intimate dyad.

Time Required: Fifteen minutes is required for administering the Family Value Profile (FVP). The remainder of the session, and future sessions, can be used to explore, discuss, and resolve value differences.

Rationale: Values are as influential in day-to-day family activities and cohesiveness as any part of family life. Often family conflict results from fundamental differences in values. Value differences may show up as power struggles, communication breakdowns, role conflicts, and generation gaps. The FVP focuses the family's attention on values, and provides an opportunity for the trainer to lead the family in an exploration of values, and in expanding plurality, tolerance, insight, and goal sharing.

Procedures: Instruct the family members to answer as they perceive the family's behavior to indicate the values. Indicate there are no right or wrong perceptions and that family growth is most likely to occur when all are honest and straightforward about their perceptions and values.

Variations: The FVP can be used as a precounseling and postcounseling instrument or as a family education tool. Although developed as a family tool, the FVP can be used with groups or dyads to facilitate cohesiveness, growth, and appreciation of differences. With modifications, a similar tool can be used in consulting with organizations, work forces, unions, and businesses.

Trainer's Notes: Values act as organizers for family time, energy, space, and resource management. Values are instrumental in the allocation of money and other resources. If a family member has little or no influence in establishing and maintaining the family's values, the result is often sabotage of family goals and family harmony. Values are abstractions which can be modified through discussions and information sharing.

The question often arises as to how much difference in values makes a problem for families. A trainer should never undertake to achieve complete agreement within a family, but focus on only the major differences. As a general principle of operation, it is usually important to focus on the one to four greatest differences. It is important to get a sense of family as a whole and then try to work on the crucial differences.

RELATIONSHIP VALUE PROFILE

Quickly read through the list of values listed below. Think of your family as a whole (unit), then rank each value as you believe your family's total behavior reflects its values. Be aware that individual family members' values vary, but the family as a whole has a hierarchy of values. Next rank the same values in terms of your personal values. Give the rank of 1 to the value which is most valued, 2 to the second most valued, and so on for each listed item. Rank all values in each list from 1 to 14.

FAMILY BEHAVIOR VALUES

_____ Appearance/looks

_____ Athletics/sports

_____ Cooperation/empathy

_____ Education

_____ Freedom/initiative

_____ Fun/happiness

_____ Health

_____ Leisure

_____ Money/security

_____ Neatness/cleanliness

_____ Religion

_____ Submission/obedience

_____ Trustworthiness/reliability

_____ Work

PERSONAL BEHAVIOR VALUES

_____ Appearance/looks

_____ Athletics/sports

_____ Cooperation/empathy

_____ Education

_____ Freedom/initiative

_____ Fun/happiness

_____ Health

_____ Leisure

_____ Money/security

_____ Neatness/cleanliness

_____ Religion

_____ Submission/obedience

_____ Trustworthiness/reliability

_____ Work

List any other values which you feel are a major force in organizing the family's time, energy, space, or distribution of resources_____

_____

_____

List any values which **YOU** think should have more priority in the family_____

_____

_____

Dyad Assessment: Accelerator and Brake

Glen Jennings
Ron McManus

Brief Description: This exercise can be used by the trainer or the couple to identify areas of the dyadic relationship that need adjustment. It can provide an index for determining the area and the amount of adjustment needed to develop a more satisfying relationship.

Objectives:
1. To assist trainers and couples in identifying specific areas of the relationship needing adjustment.
2. To provide an analogy for evaluating the severity of a problem.
3. To provide a vehicle for opening communication to problem areas of the relationship.

Materials Needed: Two copies of the Dyad Assessment: Accelerator and Brake Worksheet and pencils for each dyad.

Group Composition: The group composition is the dyad and trainer, or the dyad alone. This exercise can be used in marriage enrichment activities in which there could be a number of dyads.

Time Required: Administration time is brief (about 15 minutes). Scoring is quick and simple. Counseling (work) resulting from the assessment may be carried forth a number of sessions as specific problem areas are addressed.

Rationale: This exercise creates an analogy between marriage and an automobile. Most couples can readily identify and discuss what would happen with an automobile when the brake and accelerator were increased simultaneously or in a haphazard manner. The couple can see the ill consequences whenever the brake or accelerator were depressed without the driver or passengers being aware of the action.

Some couples experiencing unsatisfactory relationships are unaware of the problem areas of the union. This technique places problem resolution as a shared activity when the couple recognizes that one may be overaccelerating as the other is overbraking. A metaphor for the marriage is available as they discuss the dangers of fast driving or braking unexpectedly. The assessment provides an opportunity to see whether each member of the couple is experiencing the same marriage.

Procedures:

1. Introduce the exercise by talking about the analogy of a marriage relationship and an automobile in terms of the necessity of the accelerator and brake working in a cooperative manner if the auto is to progress smoothly down the road.
2. Distribute a copy of the Dyad Assessment: Accelerator and Brake Worksheet and a pencil to each person.
3. Instruct each person to read the directions and to look over the exercise. Ask if anyone has questions.
4. If there are questions, answer them to the best of your ability. If there are no questions, instruct participants to begin the exercise.
5. After the dyad(s) completes the instrument, have each of them compute their score, and then engage the dyad in a comparison of their responses and the meaning of them.
6. There are a number of options for bringing closure to the exercise:

    A. Schedule the dyad for marital counseling.
    B. Assign activities based upon the scores as home-growth (work).
    C. Continue the discussion in terms of "What if_____:"

- What if the two of you continue the present pattern; how long before the auto is wrecked?
- What if each of you plan and implement a more cooperative driving plan?
- What if_____changes but_____is too greedy to change?
- What if_____?

Variations: The assessment can be used with any dyad, or expanded to include the nuclear or extended family. With modifications, an assessment could be made of parent-child, parent-adolescent, or dating couples' dyads.

Trainer's Notes: Some items may need clarification depending upon the backgrounds of the participants. Some items may need to be eliminated depending upon the constellation of individuals involved. Caution couples of the importance of listening to their mate's concerns without becoming defensive and getting into a power struggle.

DYAD ASSESSMENT:
ACCELERATOR AND BRAKE WORKSHEET

Occasionally couples develop a pattern of either relating and working together, or of opposing each other much like the accelerator and brake of the automobile. That is, one feels as if he or she must continually be accelerating the relationship or else life would become unbearable. The other may be very content with the relationship as it is, or feel that he or she must be braking to prevent the partner from accelerating the relationship off the road. Too often, the couple may go on and on, with one accelerating or braking while the other is content. More likely, one is accelerating while the other is braking, and this often results in resentment or a continual power struggle. This brief assessment allows the couple to evaluate the degree to which the relationship is a contest of accelerating and braking. Like all assessments, this one requires frankness and honesty to be of most value.

Look at the following 13 phrases or areas of a relationship and mark on the Self Scale the degree of accelerating or braking that you feel YOU are doing. Next look at the same areas and mark on the Mate Scale the degree of accelerating or braking that you feel YOUR PARTNER is doing. For each scale, quickly write the number (from 1 to 9) which best represents how YOU FEEL about each item in terms of the accelerating or braking of the relationship: 1, 2, or 3 would mean that you feel you are often accelerating the relationship in terms of that particular area; 4, 5, or 6 would indicate that you feel the relationship is going smoothly in that area; 7, 8, or 9 would indicate that you feel you are putting much effort into braking the relationship in that particular area to keep it from running away and destroying the partnership.

1	2	3	4	5	6	7	8	9

FULL ACCELERATION   PLEASURE CRUISING   FULL BRAKING

SELF SCALE   MATE SCALE

———————— COUPLE GOALS ————————

———————— TIME SPENT TOGETHER ————————

———————— APPRECIATION OF OTHER ————————

———————— INTIMACY AND SEX ————————

———————— DIVISION OF HOUSEHOLD LABOR ————————

———————— DECISION MAKING/EQUALITY ————————

———————— FINANCES/MONEY MANAGEMENT ————————

———————— CHILD REARING ————————

———————— BOUNDARIES OF MARRIAGE ————————

———————— RELIGION ————————

———————— IN-LAW RELATIONSHIPS ————————

———————— INTERPERSONAL FLEXIBILITY ————————

———————— LEISURE ACTIVITIES ————————

Dyadic Sexual Satisfaction Inventory

Glen Jennings

Brief Description: An exercise that can be used with couples to evaluate their level of sexual satisfaction and initiate communication about the sexual area of their relationship. There are 20 areas of sexual satisfaction which each member of the couple evaluates, and an opportunity to make specific comments can lead to sexual counseling and sexual enrichment.

Objectives:
1. To assist trainers and dyads/couples in resolving sexual problems and/or identifying areas for sexual enrichment.
2. To provide a basis for initiating communication in the sexual area of dyadic relationships.

Materials Needed: Two copies of the Dyadic Sexual Satisfaction Inventory and pencils for each couple.

Group Composition: This exercise is intended to be used with couples, but under specific circumstances is valuable in individual situations.

Time Required: Administration time is brief, about 20 to 30 minutes. The discussion and counseling which would follow could range from one to eight or ten sessions.

Rationale: The sexual area of a relationship or marriage is crucial for many couples. Yet many couples tend to ignore the sexual problems and are unable to begin a growth-oriented discussion of the sexual areas of the relationship. Also, some counselors are somewhat reluctant to initiate a discussion with couples about the sexual area of the relationship. This inventory can be used to overcome either difficulty.

Procedures:
1. Give each person a copy of the Dyadic Sexual Satisfaction Inventory and a pencil.
2. Instruct that the directions are to be read and ensure that they are understood.
3. Emphasize that there are *no right or wrong answers* as long as the answers are truthful.
4. Encourage participants that comments should be made in the area provided on the Inventory.

Variations: Although the Dyadic Sexual Satisfaction Inventory was developed for use with married couples, it can be used with any dyad–cohabitators, engaged couples, gay couples, etc. By encouraging and getting dyads to make comments in the comment area, the counselor will have more information for structuring an intervention and developing a plan for sexual enrichment. Often a discussion of the results will lead to an exploration of the scripts, roles, and negative sexual messages which clients received from their families of origin, church, and peers.

Trainer's Notes: Depending upon the educational level of the clients, the counselor may need to clarify some of the items. It may be necessary for the counselor to help the couple become comfortable enough to reveal and talk about their sexuality. This can be done through rapport-building and entering into a gentle discussion about sex and one's sexuality. Some trainers use self-disclosure as a method for reducing participants' anxieties and facilitating discussion of sensitive areas.

DYADIC SEXUAL SATISFACTION INVENTORY

First, mark your level of sexual satisfaction for each item. Do not spend too much time on each item; mark your first impression. After marking the score of every item, go back and make any comment about any item which will facilitate problem solving. Keep comments brief, specific, and as behavioral as possible (e.g., Playfulness: sex is too serious, I would like to shower together, dance nude, massage each other, etc.). The sexual satisfaction score levels are as follows:

1 = much improvement desired

2 = improvement desired

3 = satisfactory

4 = very satisfactory

SCORE   **COMMENTS**

1. ___Talk related to intimacy

2. ___Setting for sex (emotional
   atmosphere, physical
   environment)

3. ___Feel appreciated by mate

4. ___Personal hygiene of mate

5. ___Foreplay and pleasuring

6. ___Approach behavior
   (the 15 to 60 minutes before
   foreplay)

7. ___Kissing (mouth-to-mouth)

8. ___Kissing (mouth-to-breasts, _____
    genitals, and other erogenous _____
    areas) _____

9. ___Playfulness of sex _____

10. ___Sense of discovery (willing- _____
    ness to experiment and _____
    talk of sexual pleasures) _____

11. ___Sexual responsiveness of _____
    mate _____

12. ___Frequency, timing, and _____
    length of intercourse _____

13. ___Sense of knowing own _____
    sexual needs _____

14. ___Use of erotica _____

15. ___Orgasmic rate _____

16. ___Nudity _____

17. ___Oral sex _____

18. ___Afterplay (the 15 to 60 _____
    minutes after sex) _____

19. ___Sense of knowing mate's _____
    sexual needs _____

20. ___Sense of feeling known _____
    and approved _____

Additional comments relating to sexual satisfaction_____

_____
_____
_____
_____

Fighting Patterns

Peggy Avent
Glen Jennings
Ron McManus

Brief Description: A simple checklist of common destructive fighting patterns which can serve as a worksheet for change.

Objective: To provide individuals with a quick, nonthreathening assessment of their fighting styles.

Materials Needed: A copy of the Worksheet and a pencil for each participant.

Group Composition: Any size group.

Time Required: Five to fifteen minutes to complete worksheet.

Rationale: When individuals assess their own fighting styles with this quick Worksheet, they are often more honest and less defensive than if confronted by others.

Procedures:
1. Open the exercise with the following comments:
   • People love a "test."
   • A worksheet offers everyone something that relates to his or her own pattern of behavior.
   • This is a "test" in which everybody wins and nobody loses. The participants: win by seriously examining their own ac-

tions; cannot lose because there are no right or wrong answers; and decide if their answers correspond to the actions they wish to display.

2. Distribute a Worksheet and a pencil to each person and ask everyone to take five minutes to answer the sheet. Responses are "yes" or "no." Ask the participants to notice the feelings they have as they complete the worksheet.

3. After five minutes, ask the participants to discuss the exercise. The trainer asks for comments, observations, and reflections. The worksheet can be discussed in the group setting since almost everyone can identify some of his or her own pattern from the checklist. The discussion is usually relaxed and often the individuals laugh about the obvious problem behaviors that they have been ignoring.

4. You may wish to highlight these points if they did not arise in the group discussion:
   - "Yes" responses on the worksheet could indicate less desirable attitudes and actions for relationships.
   - Numerous "yes" responses might suggest certain undesired patterns (e.g., taking cheap shots, giving in and holding a grudge, etc.)
   - A means of creating successful fighting might mean doing actions that would create "no" responses for the worksheet.

5. Send the group away with the worksheet and suggest that the worksheet may be used as homework for the participants.

Variations: Divide the group into small groups of five to ten members each. In the small group, members can reveal only one behavior that they recognize in themselves. The small group can discuss these behaviors.

The small group may also choose to create additional questions for the Worksheet. You may choose to give some examples of questions for reflection, such as:

- Who do you fight with the best/worst?
- What do you like about the way you fight?
- What should you change about the way you fight?
- What is most unfair about the way you fight?
- Whom do you fight with the most? Why?

- Do you fight the same with all group members?
- Do you have a special fight habitat, such as in your room or office or elsewhere?
- Do you fight someone else's fights?
- Describe "dirty fighting."

Trainer's Notes: This exercise can be modified easily to accommodate any group, e.g., a family, a group of teachers, an office or business group, etc. By giving special attention to developing an open attitude on the part of all members, the group could get into some real problem solving and groundwork for better communication patterns.

To add an element of humor which will carry a powerful long-term adjustment, arbitrarily define certain levels of behavior with names, such as: ten or more "yes" answers = "a cheap shot artist," seven to nine = "dirty Dan or dirty Darling," four to six = "Power Puss."

If the group has established close rapport, they could openly discuss the one change that they would like to see each member give attention to for improvement. This would need to be handled with a great deal of sensitivity.

WORKSHEET:
FIGHTING PATTERNS–DO YOU FIGHT FAIR?

yes   no   1. Do you say "I'm sorry" before you are ready?

yes   no   2. Do you pretend that the fight isn't important
                    or laugh about it?

yes   no   3. Do you walk out, fall asleep, or not pay
                    attention? This is the silent treatment.

yes   no   4. Do you bring up secrets about the other person
                    that you know will hurt him or her badly?

yes   no   5. When you feel cornered, do you bring up
                    things that have little to do with the argument?

yes   no   6. Do you pretend to agree with an idea that you
                    don't plan to go along with later on?

yes   no   7. Do you attack something that the other person
                    feels very strongly or cares about, such as
                    religion, kinfolk, etc?

yes   no   8. Do you tell the other person what he or she is
                    feeling? This is playing Psychiatrist.

yes   no   9. Do you hold back your love, gifts,
                    compliments, or privileges when you are mad?

yes   no   10. Do you get other people like relatives, friends,
                    or family members to take your side?

yes   no   11. Do you start an argument when you know that
                    the other person is tired, upset, depressed,
                    or busy?

yes   no   12. Do you argue about things that aren't really
                    important to avoid the real issue?

yes   no   13. Are you so determined to WIN that you don't listen or really look for a solution?

yes   no   14. Do you wait until little things become big problems before talking about them?

yes   no   15. Do you avoid disagreements at all costs?

yes   no   16. Do you bring up only negative points and avoid giving positive reinforcement?

19

What Is Important?

Laura McLachlin

Brief Description: Identifying personal values is important to self-concept as well as to family/group identity. This exercise helps group members to identify personal values and to explore how they are different from and similar to others' values.

Objectives:
1. To identify personal values.
2. To facilitate discussion about values and value tolerance.
3. To enhance group communication as participants share among themselves.

Materials Needed: Paper and pen or pencil.

Group Composition: Small or large group or family.

Time Required: Ten to 30 minutes to complete, depending upon the number in the group. More time may be necessary depending upon the depth of the discussion of values and issues related to values.

Rationale: Values are significant components of our individual makeups, as well as of how we relate to others. Identifying our own values helps us to learn about ourselves and to discover our differences and similarities in relation to other people.

Procedures:
1. Instruct the group to write down the ten most valued aspects in their lives. Answers may range from materialistic items to

intangible attributes (examples: mother, father, love, trust, care, pet, etc.). Indicate that there are no right or wrong answers.

2. Instruct participants to cross five items off their lists.
3. Next ask them to cross off three more items.
4. Participants should have two items remaining. Ask them to cross off one item leaving one last item.
5. Ask for volunteers to share what they have discovered about themselves and their values.

Variations: This exercise is best when used in larger groups of eight or more. However, it can be an effective exercise when working with smaller groups, families, or couples.

Another variation is to develop a scenario. (Example: You are going to live on a deserted island and you can take only ten possessions. What are they?)

A good way to bring closure to an exercise like this is for the trainer to make positive summary statements about the group's values.

Trainer's Notes: It is important to avoid allowing the exercise to become too negative or conflict-oriented.

If participants cannot or will not eliminate items from their lists, the trainer should randomly delete the appropriate number of items from their lists. Trainers should spend ample time processing participants' feelings as a result of the activity. Anger, fear, and resentment are common feelings brought out by this exercise.

This can be a valuable exercise when working with groups and/or families who are experiencing conflict due to value differences.

Taking Your Vital Signs

Stephen Freeman

Brief Description: By identifying all the information we possess, we are better able to improve our communication with others. Sorting out feelings, thoughts, intentions, etc., helps improve understanding of self and improves communication.

Objectives:
1. To identify all sources of information available to us.
2. To help remove limitations placed on relationships due to the exclusion of "vital" information.
3. To promote growth and improve communication with couples, families, and groups.

Materials Needed: None.

Group Composition: This exercise can be done with individuals, dyads, families, or groups. If the number of participants is large, the total group can be separated into smaller groups of four to eight members each.

Time Required: This exercise will vary in length, most likely taking about 20 minutes with dyads and up to 90 minutes with larger groups.

Rationale: By becoming aware of vital signs (information) we have about ourselves and others, we open the possibility of new experiences and growth potentials. Relationships are based on communication; communication is based on knowing what it is we want to communicate. Often, the message sent is not the message received, nor is it what was meant to begin with. This exercise requires each participant to identify her/his vital signs: senses, feelings, thoughts, intentions, and actions.

Procedures:
1. Sets the stage by introducing the five vital signs: (1) *the five senses*–sight, smell, hearing, touch, and taste; (2) *feelings*– spontaneous responses to experiences (joy, anger, sadness, frustration, happiness, etc.); (3) *thoughts*–meanings and inter- pretations (desires, wants, wishes, expectations, beliefs, etc.); (4) *intentions*–things wanted in immediate situations (wants, desires, etc.), not to be confused with what is wanted from others; and (5) *actions*–behavior, or what is being done.
2. Ask participants to identify some of the various vital signs they may have experienced in past situations and during past expe- riences.
3. Help participants to differentiate *feelings* from *thoughts* (*feel- ings* can be expressed in a single word whereas *thoughts* re- quire phrases, clauses, or sentences).
4. Next help participants differentiate *intentions* from *actions*. Becoming aware of what we do and how we do it (concrete feedback from ourselves and others) allows us to evaluate *intentions* (what we want) in light of our *actions* (behaviors). If the two are not congruent, state the *intention* and again monitor the *action* (behavior). Which is more correct?
5. Next ask participants to own their vital signs and communicate this information (to the trainer or others) using first-person statements ("I" statements) and their new awarenesses.
6. Finally, suggest that *now* they have an opportunity to improve their relationships, to reduce miscommunication, to increase growth, and to have new experiences through monitoring their vital signs.

Variations: This exercise can be enhanced dramatically by creating role-playing situations for the participants to act out. By acting out the role-playing situations, participants can check their vital signs whenever the trainer stops the role-playing activity.

Some groups might benefit from by having posters available which list the different vital signs.

The exercise could be extended and enhanced by having practice rounds of "I" statements. By practicing the rephrasing of sentences into "I" statements, the group is more likely to carry this skill into their everyday activities.

Trainer's Notes: Some participants may have difficulty differentiating their vital signs. The vital signs many need to be explained a number of different times or in different ways to help such participants. Also, role-playing, in which the vital signs are clarified, may help some to grasp a better understanding of them.

It might be helpful to have a list of sentences which can be converted rather easily into "I" statements. Such a prepared list provides opportunities for additional practice.

Be aware of any hidden agendas, such as manipulation or persuasion, which participants may have. These people will need special practice to learn to express their vital signs and deal with relationships in more direct and honest ways. Helping participants to become clear in their intentions (i.e., how intentions relate to actions) is paramount.

Strikes, Spares, Splits, and Gutterballs

Paul McDaniel

Brief Description: This exercise is based loosely on the game of bowling. Each participant takes a turn responding to a hypothetical question or problem and the other players rate his or her response as either a strike, spare, split, or gutterball. This exercise fosters better communication, creativity in problem solving, and an expansion of options in relationships within a fun/game setting.

Objectives:
1. To enhance problem-solving skills.
2. To increase communications skills.
3. To have fun while solving problems and improving relationships.

Materials Needed: Index cards with strike, spare, split, or gutterball printed on them. Each player will need all four cards; prepare enough for the size of the group. Also prepare a set of cards with hypothetical problems, situations, or questions. There will need to be enough hypothetical cards for each player to have a card for each round/frame to be played.

Group Composition: Family or group: Any number of players can participate. Players can participate as individuals, couples, or teams.

Time Required: Thirty to 90 minutes depending upon the number of players and number of frames/games to be played.

Rationale: Many people get stuck in solving problems because they lack creativity or flexibility in their thinking. By scoring players on their responses to hypothetical relational problems, this exercise fosters creativity in problem-solving by rewarding players for their creative solutions to common relational problems.

Procedures:
1. Give each player a set of four cards: one of each marked strike, spare, split, and gutterball.
2. Consult the players as to how they prefer to play–as individuals, as dyads, or as teams.
3. Determine the order of play (bowling). Players can volunteer, flip coins, or draw numbers for order of play.
4. If the choice of the group is to play as dyads, each dyad will have to determine the order of play.
5. The first player randomly selects a card from the deck of problem cards and reads it to his or her co-player(s).
6. Allow a set time for the co-player to respond. All players should have the same time limit–usually between two and eight minutes.
7. After the co-player responds to the problem card all other players each rate the response as either a strike, a spare, a split, or a gutterball. The total of the responses are recorded; strikes are 30 points, spares are 20 points, splits are 10 points, and gutterballs are 0 points.
8. All players bowl/play the predetermined number of frames/times, then the scores are totaled. The player with the highest score is the winner.

Variations: The exercise can be changed from a dyadic activity to an individual activity or to a team activity. Groups made up of couples could be divided into male/female teams. For a family or families, the players could be paired as mothers and sons, fathers and daughters, etc.

To limit the exercise in terms of competitiveness, each bowler/player may be allowed to discard the one or two lowest scores he or she receives.

If time permits, the trainer could have the group write their own hypothetical problems. Many will write relational problems they are currently experiencing or have experienced in the past. Encourage them to be creative in the writing of problems.

To discourage competition with some groups, the trainer may want to have the group discuss the problems and solutions. By discussing each problem and its many solutions, players will become cognizant of the many solutions available for each problem.

Trainer's Notes: The trainer needs to be aware of the possibility of some players placing importance on winning rather than on expanding their problem-solving skills. Often the exercise can be strengthened by briefly discussing the importance of creative thinking, cooperation, and talking about the options available when confronted with relational problems.

Help the group to see that there are no right or wrong answers, only a variation of answers. Some answers may be more appropriate than others depending upon the people involved and the specifics given.

The trainer should write an adequate number of relational problems to accommodate the playing of a number of frames/games by a number of players.

RELATIONAL PROBLEMS

The following is only a beginning list of problem situations that can be used for this exercise; the trainer should develop others as well.

1. Your mate is planning a special evening out tonight. He/she has worked long hours all week and has made it obvious that he/she is looking forward to this evening for the two of you to be alone. Late in the afternoon your mother calls to remind you about an outing she had planned for you and her. You completely forgot about it. Your mother is counting on you; your mate is counting on you. What do you do?

2. Your family would like to spend the coming holiday season at the seashore. Your 15-year-old son does not want to go; he does not want to be away from his girlfriend. The girlfriend's parents would not be open to her going with your family. How would you handle this?

3. It is your mate's birthday and he/she expects you to be home on time for an evening at the theater and dinner at a special restaurant. At 3:00 your boss assigns you a task that must be completed before 10:00 a.m. tomorrow. The task will require five to six hours of time. What do you do?

4. Your mate wants you to accompany him/her on a visit to his/her parents on Saturday. Your boss has asked you and your mate to share tickets he has to the NBA All Star Game on Saturday. What do you do?

5. At breakfast your parents call and want you to take a day off from work in order to go with them to prepare their will. You have important appointments set for the day. How would you handle this?

6. Your oldest son accuses you of letting your mate make all the decisions for the family. He wants to do something and has been told "no" by your mate. How will you respond to him?

7. As you are driving to work, it dawns on you that yesterday was your tenth wedding anniversary and you did nothing to honor your mate and the occasion. What do you do now?

8. You have scheduled a golf match for the same time as your daughter's kindergarten graduation. How will you handle this?

9. Your mate has reservations for lunch with you at an intimate restaurant near your work site. It is your birthday. You get grossly overinvolved with a project at work and time slips by; suddenly you notice that it is one hour and fifteen minutes past the appointment time. You had told the department secretary not to bother you with *any* calls. When you get home later in the day your mate refuses to talk with you. How do you work this out?

Let's Make a Picture

Lee Hipple

Brief Description: Improving decision-making skills fosters positive relationships and leads to greater productivity. Finding out who is a follower and who is a leader can be quite revealing when making a picture and solving a problem.

Objectives:
1. To help group members become more aware of their level of participation in the group.
2. To help group members become more aware of how much they are influenced by other group members.
3. To give group members a chance to use a medium other than speech for looking at the group process.

Materials Needed: Large sheets of poster paper or construction paper; crayons, felt pens, and colored pencils.

Group Composition: A family or a small group. Larger groups can be divided into subgroups of no fewer than three and no more than six members.

Time Required: Twenty to 30 minutes is the minimum amount of time required. More time is needed if there are several small groups which will be sharing with the larger group.

Rationale: Because of a tendency to become absorbed in task to the point that we ignore process, we often lack awareness of the role we play in any group of which we are a part. This exercise can help group members look at their individual roles and at how much they may be influenced by others. It can also help to increase group creativity and provide an enjoyable group experience.

Procedures:
1. Give each group a large piece of poster paper or construction paper. Have available felt pens, crayons, and colored pencils so individuals can choose which they want to use.
2. Explain that the group has 15 minutes to create a pictorial symbol of a chosen subject. The subject might be "Our Family"; or an emotion such as "Anger," "Sadness," or "Joy"; a concept, such as "Counseling," "Endings," or "Beginnings." The subject is chosen to fit in with the theme of the group or with the issues on which the group is currently working.
3. When ten minutes have passed, stop the group and ask them to take five minutes to analyze how they have been working. To guide this discussion, direct their attention to questions written (prepared in advance) on a board or large piece of paper. The questions might include, but are not limited to, the following:
   a. How are things being decided in your group?
   b. Whose ideas are being carried out?
   c. Is everyone being listened to?
   d. Is everyone in the group participating?
4. When the five minutes of discussion are up, tell the group that they have five more minutes in which to complete their project.
5. Have the group talk about their picture/symbol. If there are several groups, bring them all together and have them post their pictures around the room. Then have them explain their pictures and the ways they worked to create them.
6. After each group has shared their pictures, have them break up again into their separate groups and discuss how they worked together as a unit. Emphasize that in this discussion, all points of view should be accepted as valid because every person experiences events differently. The following questions may be posed to stimulate discussion:
   a. Were you influenced during your second work period because you had been made to stop and consider how you were working?

b. Did anyone make a decision to work differently after the discussion?

c. Does anyone wish they had worked differently in his or her group?

Variations: The questions might be changed to push the group toward looking at roles, such as: Who made decisions (about the color of paper to use, or whether crayons or felt pens were used)? Who made the decision about what to draw? If this is a family or an ongoing group, did members tend to stick to their accustomed roles within the group?

Trainer's Notes: This exercise can be helpful for families or individuals who tend to intellectualize things. It can also highlight the creativity of certain group members and may give those who are not as verbal an outlet for expression.

However, this exercise could also reinforce already established roles within the family or group, and if the trainer is not clear about the rules (i.e., that no one person's ideas are of less value, all points of view should be accepted, etc.), it could reinforce negative feelings that certain group members might have about themselves.

SECTION THREE:
DYAD/COUPLE DISCUSSION STARTERS

CHAPTER SUMMARIES

Chapter 23.   **Dyad Format**

This exercise has been suggested to dyads/couples who are experiencing considerable conflict. It comes under the category of paradoxical intention. Certain nights of the week are assigned as fight nights.

Chapter 24.   **Relationship Patterns from Family of Origin**

This exercise is based on family of origin theory and helps dyads/couples get in touch with patterns of behavior learned from their parents. The exercise is in sentence completion form, with the sentence stems focusing upon one's parents and family of origin.

Chapter 25.   **Circle of Power**

This exercise helps couples to become more nurturing of themselves and their significant others. The circle of objects from nature is used to remind each to nurture each other.

Chapter 26.   **Dyad Dialogue**

An exercise designed to help dyads/couples improve communication, develop more intimacy, and learn a skill–dialoguing. During the exercise couples return to a dating type behavior–eye intimacy, hand holding, and open-ended talking.

Chapter 27.   Turning a Quiet Trick

Passing compliments back and forth based upon the card game of Blackjack is a quiet way to improve an intimate relationship.

Chapter 28.   The Song of Relationships

Most relationships and especially dyads can be symbolized and discussed as a variation of popular music–classical, easy listening, folk, country western, light rock, hard rock, etc. In this exercise, couples select songs from their favorite kinds of music to metaphorically represent the *best* and *worst* of their relationships. The exercise allows dyads to discuss their relationships in a humorous yet meaningful way. This often results in changes in the relationship without the hurt and degradation that results from open conflict and power struggles.

Chapter 29.   Sexual Myth Deflator Exercise

The groups/dyads are given a list of prevalent sexual myths. The dyads use the list as a discussion starter to correct erroneous information, to self reveal, and to become more intimate and comfortable with their sexuality.

Chapter 30.   Close Encounters

Partners recall through the eyes of each other three events that required extreme levels of support from the other and thereby enhance each one's sense of how well their relationships has worked

Chapter 31.   Dreaming

Dyad members create a dream for the relationship, then as a dyad they try to create a dream that combines the best of the two separate dreams. Often while dreaming, creative solutions can be uncovered which help with everyday problems.

Chapter 32.   Say It Softly So I Can Hear You

Becoming a better listener is a sure way to become a better communicator and a better mate, whether work mate or intimate mate.

Chapter 33.   Quiet Reflections

This exercise promotes spirituality in couples and individuals, and creates a sense of caring and appreciation. It does not emphasize a specific belief system, but rather enhances a sense of spirituality. The dyad or couple is most likely to have a greater sense of "being a couple" after completing the exercise.

Chapter 34.   Wisdom of the Aged

Young couples often lack the resources that could make a difference in their relationships. This exercise helps develop one resource which could make a difference. By pairing older and younger couples good things often happen.

Chapter 35.   Why Do I Love You

By reacquainting couples with why they fell in love, the spark can often be rekindled and the fires roar again. Boredom kills more relationships than any other thing. This exercise helps couples to rediscover their love for each other.

Dyad Format

Charles F. Kemp
Ron McManus
Glen Jennings

Brief Description: This exercise has been suggested to dyads/couples who are experiencing considerable conflict. It comes under the category of paradoxical intention. Certain nights of the week are assigned as fight nights.

Objectives:
1. To reduce the amount of conflict in a relationship.
2. To introduce humor as a problem-solving tool.

Materials Needed: Copies of the Fight Contract.

Group Composition: One or more couples or dyads.

Time Required: Brief (15 to 30 minutes).

Rationale: Relationships often come to an impasse, and the people involved do not know what to do to break the impasse; often it becomes an ongoing argument or power struggle. This exercise shows the participants how to resolve such power struggles by deliberately planning a time to argue.

Procedures:
1. Begin the exercise by making a few opening remarks:
   • People often feel helpless when disagreements or conflicts arise.

- People feel better if they feel they are working to improve a situation.
- Individuals, and particularly couples, would rather work together toward a goal than to work against each other.

2. Ask the participants to group into dyads.
3. Each dyad is to discuss how they handle conflicts (allow about five minutes).
4. Then offer the following suggestions:
   - Imagine you are actually in a conflict with your partner.
   - Agree between the two of you to set aside three nights of the week as conflict nights, e.g., Monday, Wednesday, and Friday. On the three nights selected, you can shout, scream, and argue as much as you want. The only limitation is that you cannot engage in physical violence.
   - On the other nights, there is a moratorium on fighting. Whatever comes up must wait until a fight night.
5. Ask the group to discuss how this exercise would work for them. After the discussion, each receives a copy of the Fight Contract.
6. Conclude by suggesting that the individuals use the exercise in their relationships. The contract would be used as a means of agreeing to use the format.

Variations: This exercise can be used successfully with any dyad or group who finds themselves in continual power struggles. It is especially helpful with husbands and wives, parents and children, and parents and adolescents.

Trainer's Notes: The trainer should be knowledgeable and comfortable using paradoxical methods before using this exercise.

FIGHT CONTRACT

We (_____ & _____) agree to set aside three days
(_____, _____, & _____) as official conflict nights. The
other days of the week are off-limits for arguments, conflicts, sarcasm, and negativism.

We agree to use this format for _____weeks.

This contract is implemented today_____.
(date)

Signed,

_____

_____

Relationship Patterns from Family of Origin

Glen Jennings

Brief Description: This exercise is based on family of origin theory and helps dyads/couples get in touch with patterns of behavior learned from their parents. The exercise is in sentence completion form, with the sentence stems focusing upon one's parents and family of origin.

Objectives:
1. To open family of origin issues for discussion.
2. To help couples and others to identify behavior patterns from their families of origin.
3. To reduce conflict by opening discussion of behavior patterns that may irritate others.

Materials Needed: The Family of Origin Marital Sentence Stems Worksheet and pencils for each participant.

Group Composition: Usually limited to the dyad and the counselor. However, the exercise, with modifications, can be used by groups not limited to couples.

Time Required: Typically 30 to 60 minutes for the actual exercise. The exercise most likely will lead to a number of counseling sessions as family of origin issues develop.

Rationale: Many couples tend to repeat their parents' marriages. It appears to matter little whether the marriages were good or bad; and if they were bad, they may not serve the current generation well. This activity leads couples in an examination and discussion of how they may be repeating their parents' relationships. Couples who are less differentiated from their parents are most likely to repeat their parents' relationships, and are most likely to experience relationship problems. For married couples, identifying destructive patterns of repetition may help them begin the process of creating their own marriages and differentiating from their parents' marriages.

Procedures:
1. Introduce the activity by giving a brief explanation of family of origin. The explanation should be built around the following ideas:
   - Our first learnings occur in the family and are about the family.
   - The first models of marriage, interpersonal relationships, and family are often powerful influences; these may be part of our behaviors and thought processes throughout life unless special effort is put forth to become free of these forces.
   - Due to the preconscious aspects of how we learn "to do family," it usually requires special effort to consciously make changes in behaviors learned in our families of origin.
   - The more the child is triangulated between parents at an early age, the more likely family loyalties will develop.
   - Family loyalties are repeated whether they serve us well or not, and operate at a less than conscious level.
   - Family loyalties are most likely to function as self talk, scripts, beliefs, and behaviors that would not be repeated if we were free to observe our behaviors at a greater distance.
   - Differentiating is the process of breaking family loyalties in such a way that we become our own persons and can more consciously select the things from our families of origin that we want to repeat.
2. Point out that the more differentiated from our families of origin we become, the less we will feel like small children when in the presence of our parents and families.
3. Give all participants a copy of The Family of Origin Marital Sentence Stems Worksheet and a pencil.

4. Instruct everyone to read the directions for completing the Worksheet. After allowing enough time for all to read the directions, ask if there are any questions. If there are no questions, tell the participants to begin.
5. After all have had time to complete the Worksheet, tell them to look back over their papers and make some summary statements about patterns they may be repeating from the family of origin.
6. Encourage participants to identify any themes which are evident. Ask if they can note any differences and similarities resulting from their parents' marriages.
7. Encourage all to develop a plan for reducing problems which may have developed in their own marriages.

Variations: Although this exercise tends to focus mostly on the negatives from the family of origin, it can be varied to focus on the positives or healthy aspects of parents' marriages. Also, the trainer can eliminate or add sentence stems to fit the particular situation or couple.

One variation may be to develop stems around specific themes, e.g., "how my parents fought," "how to be sick in my family," "family of origin and work," "children's roles in family of origin," "health in family of origin," "time in my family of origin," etc.

A variation of this exercise is to complete it while thinking of the same-sex parent, and then redo it thinking of the opposite-sex parent. This can be helpful in two ways: (1) sometimes children bond with the opposite-sex parent so they may take on that parents loyalties, and (2) completing the exercise by thinking of the opposite-sex parent may shed light on what behaviors may be expected of the mate and what behaviors may cause problems with the mate.

Trainer's Notes: The 25 sentence stems are related to the influence of family of origins, and are arranged by themes in groups of five: numbers 1 through 5 focus on emotions, especially anger; 6 through 10 look at intimacy and sex; 11 through 15 focus on roles; 16 through 20 spotlight the value of money; and 21 through 25 tap rituals in the family of origin. The most meaningful aspect of this exercise is the last section, the *Summary of Learning* statements.

To really get into family of origin issues, it may be helpful to look back to grandparents' marriages and note how patterns are repeated over generations. Often couples can see how their parents repeated some patterns from their grandparents. This will make it easier for them to see how they may be repeating things from their parents.

This activity can be more powerful by directing the couple to mimic (posture, speech, etc.) one of the couple's parents. Then at the next session, mimic the other set of parents.

If the trainer/counselor has worked with the couple for a few sessions, the stems can be modified so that problems will be more spotlighted and lead to more specific problem resolution.

Some people have great difficulty being critical of their parents. This is evidence of their being stuck in their family of origin. For such people it may help to point out that, *"only when we can criticize can we love fully!"*

FAMILY OF ORIGIN MARITAL
SENTENCE STEMS WORKSHEET

Directions: Go through the list of incomplete sentences, writing in your same-sex parent (father or mother) in the first blank, and then completing the sentence with the first phrase that comes to mind. There are no right or wrong answers, so simply try to give the most frank answers.

1. When my_____was angry, he/she would_____

2. To hurt others_____would_____

3. My_____'s pet peeve with mother/father was_____

4. To_____, a good time meant_____

5. To_____, fighting was_____

6. _____showed his/her love to mother/father by_____

7. When my_____wanted sex, he/she would_____

8. Sex to_____was_____

9. To_____, love meant_____

10. _____felt most intimate_____

11. My_____saw children as_____

12. To_____, a father was_____

13. To_____, daughters were_____

14. _____thought mothers were_____

15. To_____, sons were_____

16. To_____, money was_____

17. _____thought a good use of money was_____

18. _____spent foolish money on_____

19. _____'s favorite comment about money was_____

20. Savings to_____represented_____

21. Holidays were to_____like_____

22. _____'s favorite ritual of the holidays was_____

23. Most holidays to_____meant_____

24. To_____, the house was_____

25. _____thought our family should always_____

Summary of Learnings

After looking over sentences 1 through 5, which are related to emotions from family of origin, make a summary statement._____

_____

Sentences 6 through 10 reveal patterns regarding intimacy and sex from family of origin. Write a summary statement about love and sex._____

_____

Family of origin roles are portrayed by sentences 11 through 15. What summary statement is indicated?_____

_____

_____

Money patterns (sentences 16 through 20) from family of origin can be summarized by the following statement:

_____

_____

Family rituals are revealed by sentences 21 through 25; a summary statement is_____

_____

_____

Circle of Power

Ajakai Jaya

Brief Description: This exercise helps couples to become more nurturing of themselves and their significant others. The circle of objects from nature is used to remind each to nurture each other.

Objectives:
1. To offer the opportunity for couples to support one another.
2. To offer an experience in which nurturing of self and others is appropriate.
3. To build group cohesiveness.

Materials Needed: Objects from nature such as leaves, rocks, twigs, pebbles, flowers, logs, bones, remains, etc.

Group Composition: Dyads of spouses, friends, or lovers. Any number of dyads may participate, but if the group is very large (more than eight pairs), the group can be divided into smaller groups of three to eight pairs.

Time Required: The specific exercise may take 30 to 60 minutes. The time required can be extended easily depending upon the depth of the experience to which the group wants to carry it.

Rationale: Often due to the busy and stressful lives many people live, it is difficult to nurture oneself and one's significant other. It is also difficult to take the time to look inside oneself in order to get more in touch with one's own strengths and positive factors. This exercise offers an opportunity to nurture oneself and one's significant other.

The concept of Circle of Power should be well thought out by the trainer before the group comes together. Analogies that can be made are the Native Americans living in circular camps and the pioneers circling up the wagon trains for the night. A circle tends to bring people together in such a way that everyone is facing each other. A circle fosters better communication, more closeness, and encourages greater nurturing of others. It creates a sense of togetherness. Many groups through history have used the circle as a special or sacred place.

Procedures:
1. Discuss with the group the idea of a circle of power. Lay out the area to be designated as the circle of power and point this place out to the group.
2. Gather objects from nature either before beginning the exercise, or make this a part of the exercise.
3. Instruct participants to go to the nature objects and select one item which has special meaning to them. Suggest that they are to find symbolic power in the object they select.
4. Have them return with their special object to the site selected to be the circle of power.
5. Have each person place his or her special object inside the circle of power. Then have each person tell his or her significant other the special meaning the object holds for him or her.
6. Close the exercise by reminding everyone of humans' relatedness to nature and to one another.
7. The circle of power can be preserved as a place for meditation, thought, or prayer.

Variations: This is an excellent exercise for groups on retreats for marriage enrichment. It is open to many different variations. It seems to be a more powerful exercise when the participants go into the woods to gather their own objects/symbols.

If time permits, it can be beneficial to have dyads share the meanings of their objects with the group after having shared their meanings with their significant others. Some groups have found it helpful to provide positive feedback after the personal sharing with each other in dyads.

Another variation is to designate the circle of power as a sacred place to be preserved for a specific time period. If the group is to be together for a length of time, they may return to this special place often, either as a group, as dyads, or individually to meditate or pray, or simply to think.

Trainer's Notes: Depending upon the group involved, the trainer can make this a deeply singular religious activity, or vary it to encompass different religions. It can be a nonreligious activity. Although this is especially meaningful if conducted in a natural setting, it can be effective in many different settings. The trainer should give special effort to keeping the exercise positive and meaningful. If some members have difficulty being either positive or serious, the trainer may need to explain that the purpose of the exercise is for enhancing self-power and for nurturing of oneself and others.

Dyad Dialogue

Ron McManus
Glen Jennings

Brief Description: An exercise designed to help dyads/couples improve communication, develop more intimacy, and learn a skill–dialoguing. During the exercise couples return to a dating type behavior–eye intimacy, hand holding, and open-end talking.

Objectives:
 1. To increase the quantity and quality of dyad/couple talk.
 2. To assist dyads/couples in conveying a sense of "I care about you!"

Materials Needed: Two moveable chairs.

Group Composition: The couple; this activity can be used as part of a group activity. One couple would demonstrate the use of Dyad Dialogue for the group, then others could do the activity under the direction of the trainer.

Time Required: Approximately 30 to 45 minutes.

Rationale: Many couples over time drift into a stale relationship. Often their interactions become so mundane–with work, children, home maintenance, and the general world condition–that they lose the spark or romance of their relationship. This activity returns the relationship to date-like behavior by setting aside a specific time for each other.

Although not all relationships could be enhanced by increasing the communication which occurs, most dyadic relationships can be improved by improving the communication aspects. This activity provides a model for improving both the quantity and quality of communication in the dyad. Communication is the basis for knowing another person. As we self-reveal and communicate at a more genuine level, we will know more about ourselves as well as the other person. This exercise provides an opportunity to establish more intimacy through better communication.

Procedures:

1. Instruct everyone to think back to his/her dating days.
2. Say, "Most likely these were good days with a great feeling of love, wanting to be together, and time spent communicating with each other. Now, I want you to place the two chairs close together facing each other."
3. "Sit facing each other close enough to hold hands."
4. "Look into each other's eyes. Much of romance is conveyed through the eyes–'The *eye* is the mirror of the *soul*.' Feelings and moods are communicated through the eyes. Sensuality and sexual interest are closely aligned to eyes and eye expressions."
5. "Hold hands and send messages of love and caring. Touch is one of the most effective means of communicating feelings of affection. Continue looking into your partner's eyes while giving his/her hands a massage."
6. "After five to ten minutes of 'eye kissing' and holding hands, instruct them to ask each other some open-ended questions. Open-ended questions should elicit answers about feelings and beliefs. Examples are: What are you feeling now? If you could take a vacation, where would you like to go and what would you do? What makes you feel good about yourself? What is happiness to you? What is love? What is friendship? Open-ended questions have no right or wrong answers nor can they be answered with one word (no! yes!) responses.
7. After all have had an opportunity to experience the exercise, ask: "What are you feeling now?" "How could this exercise strengthen your relationship?" Encourage them with: "If this has been

helpful, develop a plan to use it periodically to enhance your relationship."

Variations: If facilities for videotaping are available, a videotape and playback of the exercise can be very beneficial to the couple. Have the couple note their body language on the playback.

Some dyads who have difficulty talking to each other may benefit by having a list of open-ended questions available. Such couples often have a history of talking only about specifics and responding with only short answers.

With some dyads, it may be beneficial to start by having them sit with their backs to each other. This can impress upon them the importance of body language, facial expressions, and eye contact as means of improving communication and especially of conveying affection.

Trainer's Notes: A dyad's interaction style as they do this exercise can be used as an assessment tool for other work to do in counseling. This is an excellent activity to assign as daily home growth (work).

This exercise can easily lead into opportunities for teaching or doing workshops about other communications skills. The exercise benefits group members in the following areas: (1) reflective listening skills, (2) sending "I messages," and (3) the art of checking out messages.

Some dyads may need to be cautioned to be non-evaluative and to be positive as they attempt to change some less-effective communication behaviors. Emphasize that most excellent communicators are nonjudgmental and good listeners; poor communicators often think about their responses as others are speaking.

This exercise is most likely to be effective if dyads will set a specific time to do the activity at regular intervals, e.g., Tuesday and Thursday evenings for about 20 to 30 minutes, or Monday and Wednesday mornings for 20 to 30 minutes. Caution participants that, at first, practicing the exercise may feel awkward, but that the reward of enhanced relationships is worth it. Encourage them to practice the exercise for a set time, for example, for four to six weeks.

In training sessions, it is crucial that the trainer provide a model for dyads and families. Many clients will quickly start modeling the behaviors and attitudes of the counselor. The trainer should exhibit good communications skills, be a keen listener, and show sensitivity in leading all workshops, especially this one.

27

Turning a Quiet Trick

Ajakai Jaya

Brief Description: Passing compliments back and forth based upon the card game of Blackjack is a quiet way to improve an intimate relationship.

Objectives:
1. To help focus on how we are helpful to each other.
2. To facilitate communication and appreciation.
3. To set the possibilities for further acts of helpfulness.

Materials Needed: A deck of playing cards.

Group Composition: This exercise is for a single couple/dyad, but can be adapted easily to a group or a family.

Time Required: Five to 30 minutes for a dyad; the time will vary with groups or families depending upon the time available and number of participants.

Rationale: This exercise helps dyads to take a small amount of time in their busy schedules to focus on how they help each other. By using playing cards, the dyad can move directly to identifying how they help each other. They can set the stage for future help by reminding each other of past times of being helpful.

Procedures:
1. This exercise follows the steps of the card game Blackjack. If participants do not know the rules/steps for playing Blackjack, review the steps or provide copies of the steps.

2. Two cards are dealt to each partner. As in Blackjack, each looks at his/her pair of cards and leaves the others face down. Each partner either decides to keep the two cards or requests another card. Cards are then turned to see face value. The partner with the highest card wins and the other partner rewards him/her by recalling a helpful moment from the past week. A specific example should be given of when the other was helpful.
3. Cards are redealt; step 2 is repeated as many times as desired.
4. When the exercise is completed each participant can select his/her most meaningful card to use as a follow-up procedure. As a follow-up, each person can hide his/her most meaningful card somewhere where the other person will find it in the coming week. This would help both of them to be reminded of each other's help and most likely promote continued helpfulness and appreciation. Hiding cards in places where they will be found establishes an air of good feeling and appreciation.

Variations: If the participants are not familiar with Blackjack, the exercise can be simplified to one-, two-, or three-card draw.

Another variation is to draw cards to see which one will talk about something they would like to receive (behaviorally) in the future from the other person.

Participants can be encouraged to use what they have shared in creative ways such as making posters, signs, or symbolic representations as reminders of how they help each other. They may use these in public or more private ways depending upon their own ideas.

Trainer's Notes: Although this is a rather simple idea, it can be quite useful in building a more positive relationship. Some who are of a negative bent may need extra encouragement to keep this exercise on a positive note. If some negativism enters into the exercise, the trainer may want to process with the participants their need to focus on the negative and to be negative.

28

The Song of Relationships

Glen Jennings

Brief Description: Most relationships and especially dyads can be symbolized and discussed as a variation of popular music–classical, easy listening, folk, country western, light rock, hard rock, etc. In this exercise, couples select songs from their favorite kinds of music to metaphorically represent the *best* and *worst* of their relationships. The exercise allows dyads to discuss their relationships in a humorous yet meaningful way. This often results in changes in the relationship without the hurt and degradation that results from open conflict and power struggles.

Objectives:
1. To provide a "new" way for a couple to talk about their relationship.
2. To bring about changes in the relationship by way of unconscious action.
3. To stimulate an open discussion of expectations for the relationship and the mate.

Materials Needed: With many couples, no materials other than pen and paper are required; for other dyads, it may be advantageous to have extensive lists of songs or recordings available for stimulation.

Group Composition: The dyad is the intended focus; this activity can be used quite easily with families or other groups, e.g., an office pool, a sports team, dating couples, two friends, three generations, a work force, etc.

Time Required: Typically, 30 to 60 minutes.

Rationale: Popular music is such a part of our culture that it goes with us wherever we go–to work, indoors, outdoors, lunch, dinner, shopping, and even to bed. Music and songs reflect the whole range of human emotions, from joy to disappointment, as well as our hopes and expectations. Music shapes our every behavior. This exercise allows couples to set their relationships to their favorite kinds of music. Symbolically, music and their relationships will go with them everywhere they go, thus they can keep their relationships with them, and keep them fine-tuned and more rewarding. Many dyads can easily see the analogy of how relationships must continually be tuned due to changing circumstances, much like many instruments need to be tuned as the weather changes.

Procedures:
1. Set the stage by talking about how popular music and songs (lyrics) reflect the human condition, family, men, women, roles, expectations, disappointments, and especially marriage, love, sex, and intimate relationships. It will be advantageous to have some examples of music available to share with the participants.
2. Ask the participants to identify some songs which reflect relationships of couples.
3. Now ask them to identify some songs which describe their current relationships. Allow about five to ten minutes for them to write down the titles or words from songs that characterize both the positives and the negatives of their relationships.
4. Next ask them to share these.
5. Ask them what they would like to keep as parts of the current relationships and what parts they would like to discard.
6. Finally, dump the discussion in their laps by suggesting that they have heard each others' pleas, through songs, as to what each other would like the relationship to be like, and that *NOW,* each of them has the opportunity to show how much he or she values the relationship by joining together to make a rich and rewarding duet.

Variations: Rather than focusing on the current relationship, the trainer can have the group/couples focus simply on songs which portray how they would like the relationship to be in the future. Occasionally there may be some value in talking about how the relationship was at some time in the past.

Some couples have been helped by encouraging them to write their own lyrics for their relationship or for what their relationship should become.

Trainer's Notes: Be aware of any negative drift to the exercise; stop and deal with the negatives in a session before returning to this exercise. Occasionally a couple may come along who is unaware of the richness in which music reflects the human condition. It may be beneficial to have recordings they can listen to in developing their relationship album or collection. A list of popular songs may be helpful to get some couples into the exercise. Another approach which has proven helpful is to assign the couple to listening to music together for an hour a day for a week, as a part of their home growth (work), and to then compile and bring in a list of songs that are symbolic of their relationship.

Sexual Myth Deflator Exercise

Ron McManus

Brief Description: The groups/dyads are given a list of prevalent sexual myths. The dyads use the list as a discussion starter to correct erroneous information, to self-reveal, and to become more intimate and comfortable with their sexuality.

Objectives:
1. To open a discussion about intimacy and sexuality.
2. To understand that there are "sexual myths."
3. To check whether the myth has been harmful.
4. To begin the process of correcting the myth.
5. To help couples achieve greater intimacy in their relationships.

Materials Needed: A copy of the The Sexual Myth List for each participant. Pens should be available for those who may want to make notes regarding what is the "truth."

Group Composition: This exercise can be used with couples or with a group.

Time Required: This exercise typically takes about 45 minutes with a couple or small (two- to eight-member) group.

Rationale: Sexual myths are fables or legends of heritage, embodying the convictions of a person. In a loose sense, a sexual myth can be understood as an invented story that is used to explain or rationalize certain behavior. Often the myth may have started with a small element of fact, but has been enlarged and distorted over time. This invented story or explanation is often an ill-founded belief held uncritically by a person. The sexual myths have been upheld and unchallenged for so long that they now appear to be factual. Myths need to be examined and talked about to free people to achieve more satisfaction in relationships.

Procedures:
1. Begin by making the following comments to the couple/group:
   - Sexual myths persist in all cultures.
   - Sexual myths often have a negative effect on intimate relationships.
   - Sexual myths can be examined and changes can be made based on more accurate information.
2. Instruct the group to organize itself into dyads.
3. Distribute copies of The Sexual Myth List.
4. Each dyad is to read over the list and discuss each myth. They should use the following guide to direct the discussion:
   - What is the myth?
   - How has the myth been harmful to people?
   - How has the myth been allowed to persist?
   - How has the myth affected my relationships?
   - What are the correct facts regarding the topic?
   - What changes are called for now that I have more accurate information?
5. Reconvene the group and lead an open discussion focus on the following questions:
   - What was it like for you to talk about sexual myths?
   - Did the subject matter make you feel uncomfortable? Tell us about it.
   - What did you gain by doing the exercise?

Variations: The myth being discussed can be written on an adhesive label and stuck onto an inflated balloon. When the dyad feels they have successfully worked through the myth, they symbolically burst the balloon, thereby deflating the myth.

Trainer's Notes: To put participants at ease, the trainer may want to have a poster with other sexual myths written on it. By discussing the other myths, the trainer can help others to be more comfortable with the subject of sexuality.

Sometimes a display of sexuality books can help participants to feel more at ease and more willing to enter a discussion on sexuality.

THE SEXUAL MYTH LIST

Working Myths

1. Alcohol is a sexual stimulant.
2. The desire for sexual intercourse decreases markedly after the age of 50.
3. It is dangerous to have sexual intercourse during menstruation.
4. Each person has a limited number of sexual outlets and once those are used up, sexual activity is finished.
5. Vasectomy kills a man's sex drive.
6. Menopause or hysterectomy terminates a woman's sex life.
7. Nothing can be done to help people who have a sex problem.
8. Excessive sexual activities can lead to mental breakdowns.
9. Masturbation can lead to various physical problems.

Personal Discomfort Myths

1. I am embarrassed in the nude.
2. A person should not have to talk about what pleases him/her sexually; it should occur naturally.
3. I do not feel good about my body.
4. My early sexual socialization was too guilt-ridden.
5. My religion creates sexual shame in me.
6. I get easily embarrassed talking about sex.
7. I don't know how to ask for what I want in sex.
8. Too often I feel sex is dirty and disgusting.
9. I wish I could be more playful and spontaneous in expressing my sexuality.

Close Encounters

Ajakai Jaya

Brief Description: Partners recall through the eyes of each other three events that required extreme levels of support from the other and thereby enhance each ones' sense of how well their relationship has worked.

Objectives:
    1. To develop a greater sense of support for each other.
    2. To enhance communication in the dyad.
    3. To increase appreciation of self and other.

Materials Needed: None. However, appropriate background music may enhance the exercise.

Group Composition: A dyad, or a group or family divided into dyads.

Time Required: Ten to 30 minutes.

Rationale: This exercise focuses participants' attentions on how they support each other. It helps them to become more aware of their relationships and how each contributes to their successes. The exercise tends to help dyads to reduce the pull to take each other for granted.

Procedures:
    1. Opening comments may include about how often relationships are eroded by people taking each other for granted and by assumptions being made about each other and the relationship.

2. Divide the group or family into dyads. If there is one person left alone, this person can be asigned to some dyad, or have him/her imagine a partner.
3. Partners sit opposite one another in a quiet place. Soft music may be used for background; no interruptions are allowed.
4. Designate one in each dyad as Partner A and the other as Partner B. Instruct the partners to make eye contact.
5. Partner A listens as Partner B identifies times in the last few days when Partner A was supportive of Partner B.
6. Encourage each to identify at least three specific times when the other was supportive, and to identify specific behaviors at the time.
7. Partner B now listens as Partner A does the same, by identifying three times and three specific behaviors when Partner B was supportive of Partner A.
8. Bring closure to the exercise by letting volunteers tell what they felt and what the exercise meant to them. Talk about the importance of mutual support and caring.

Variations: This exercise can be used in a work setting to increase a sense of cooperativeness and to increase morale. It can also be used in a classroom with children or adolescents.

The exercise can be followed up by encouraging each dyad to make a small sign or poster to display in their shared area to remind them of the exercise and their investment in each other. It can also be useful to post such signs or posters where all can see them.

Trainer's Notes: Caution the group that this is to be a positive experience and is not a time to air dirty laundry or confront about a lack of support. It may be helpful to remind the group that many behaviorists suggest that it takes ten to 20 positives to overcome the impact of one negative.

It may be necessary to extend the time frame in which the dyads think; some may have difficulty in identifying specific supportive behaviors over the past few days.

This activity can be helpful to couples, family member pairs, or co-workers.

Dreaming

Glen Jennings

Brief Description: Dyad members create a dream for the relationship, then as a dyad they try to create a dream that combines the best of the two separate dreams. Often while dreaming, creative solutions can be uncovered which help with everyday problems.

Objectives:
1. To promote dyadic communication and problem solving.
2. To assist dyads to form more common goal orientations.
3. To help coordinate individual expectations and experiences into a shared dream.

Materials Needed: Pens, pencils, crayons, colored chalk, and large sheets of paper (12 × 18 or larger).

Group Composition: This exercise can be used with any group as long as it can be organized into small groups or dyads.

Time Required: Thirty to 60 minutes is appropriate with most groups.

Rationale: Dreams tend to liberate individuals and groups to talk and think creatively about any idea or thing. Dreams allow us to face and resolve issues that may be off limits during our waking hours. By engaging the dyad or group in dream-making at a symbolic and metaphorical level, the trainer can assist the dyad or group in working out issues and problems that might be impossible in other ways.

Procedures:
1. Begin by explaining the following:
   - Dreams allow us to be freer than we typically are in our thinking.
   - Dreams allow us to solve problems which may be too complex to be resolved during waking hours.
2. Instruct the group to form dyads, if necessary. Each dyad should receive materials for drawing or coloring their dream.
3. Instruct all to relax by leaning back, taking a few deep breaths, relaxing each major body part one part at a time, getting into a sleepy state by having heavy eyelids, and thinking only pleasant thoughts.
4. As they are relaxed, they are to dream of what they would like their relationships to be like. After a few moments they are too begin drawing their dreams. Allow a short time for drawing the dream.
5. Now they are to explain their dreams to the other person in the dyad.
6. After each person in the dyad has explained his or her dream, the dyad members are to draw their joint dream using the best of the individual dreams.
7. For closure, the dyads are to explain very briefly their joint dreams.

Variations: A nice option with this exercise is to use it with groups of three to six people or family members. If groups are larger than six, it becomes difficult for all to be involved in the processes that occur.

Another variation is to use scrap paper, scissors, glue, paste, sticks, etc. for the construction of the dream. With some groups it may be more appropriate to bypass the individual dream and go directly to a group or family dream.

This exercise can be quite revealing when used with a work group or departmental group. The trainer can learn much about the inner workings of the group or dyad simply by observing: Who is the real manager of the group? What alliances are there in the group? How does the group or dyad communicate? How do they handle tension?

What about the distribution of power? What are the different roles in the group, dyad, or family?

Trainer's Notes: Dream work can be enjoyable and stimulating. But be prepared that at times there may be a group member who discounts any benefit from such dreaming. Such an individual often resists by pushing reality and by insisting that there are no solutions to his or her problems.

32

Say It Softly So I Can Hear You

Ajakai Jaya

Brief Description: Becoming a better listener is a sure way to become a better communicator and a better mate, whether work mate or intimate mate.

Objectives:
1. To identify specific behaviors that improve listening.
2. To improve communication skills and especially listening skills.
3. To open dialogue about communication styles and skills.

Materials Needed: Pencils and 5 × 8 index cards.

Group Composition: A couple, group, or family.

Time Required: Fifteen to 30 minutes with smaller groups or families.

Rationale: One of the surest ways to improve communication is to improve listening skills. This exercise focuses on specific ways to improve listening skills. Each partner in a dyad identifies ways in which he or she gets others to listen to him or her, and then shares these behaviors with his or her partner. This focuses attention on how to be a better listener. Some communication specialists say that improving listening skills can result in a 60-75 percent improvement in communication.

Procedures:
1. Talk briefly about the importance of better communication, and especially about the importance of better listening as the main road to better communication.

2. Instruct each person to write down several ways he/she gets others to listen. Allow time for each person to write down several items.
3. Have partners trade their lists. Then have each identify and circle one item on the other's card. It should be an item which he/she would like the partner to use with him/her.
4. Instruct them to write beside the circled item the percentage of time they are hopeful the behavior will occur in their interactions.
5. Bring closure by briefly reviewing some standards of etiquette in good communication.

Variations: A master list of the items could be made to help all improve their listening skills. A poster could be made of some of the items and posted in a conspicuous place. Another variation could be to post one item at a time at regular intervals.

This can be done as a group exercise rather than as a dyadic exercise. The trainer may want to list the items as the group identifies them.

Trainer's Notes: The trainer may need to remind the group that only positive ways of getting another's attention are acceptable. It may be necessary for the trainer to identify a few items to get the group into the exercise (examples: "I wait until the other person is through talking before I begin." "I make eye contact with the other person before I begin to talk." "I use his/her name to address him/her." "I am listening rather than thinking of a reply as the other person talks.").

33

Quiet Reflections

Ajakai Jaya

Brief Description: This exercise promotes spirituality in couples and individuals, and creates a sense of caring and appreciation. It does not emphasize a specific belief system, but rather enhances a sense of spirituality. The dyad or couple is most likely to have a greater sense of "being a couple" after completing the exercise.

Objectives:
1. To foster a sense of spirituality.
2. To help develop a greater appreciation of self and of nature.
3. To enhance the sense of being a couple for each dyad.
4. To help participants become more comfortable with silence and to recognize the therapeutic value of silence.

Materials Needed: None.

Group Composition: Couples, paired co-workers, a family, or a group. A group or family may need to be divided into pairs for the exercise. If there is an odd number of participants one unit can have three people, or the extra person can participate without a partner.

Time Required: Forty-five to 90 minutes.

Rationale: Too often, couples, family members, and co-workers do not take the time to reflect upon the importance of their relationships and what they mean to each other. This exercise provides couples/participants with a specific and structured time for enhancing spiritualness, appreciation, cooperativeness, and dialogue.

Procedures:

1. Briefly talk about the importance of spirituality and cooperation in terms of one's personal life as well as in a dyad. Often the absence of specific times for spirituality erodes a couple's sense of connectedness and spirituality.
2. Pair the participants into dyads, if necessary.
3. Instruct them that this is a specific time in which they can block out intrusions and each focus on self, significant other, and spirituality.
4. Emphasize the importance of silence and peace in their mind as they do the exercise.
5. Then instruct the dyads to split apart and to go on a walk, preferably in the woods, park, or along a beach. They are to walk in complete silence. Establish a time for all to return to the group.
6. Each participant is to find at least one item to be symbolic of the positive aspects of his or her relationship.
7. When the participants come back together, they are to recount their experiences and the symbolic interpretations of the items they have collected.

Variations: If the setting does not provide for a nature walk, the members can be instructed to go to some favorite places in their minds and to fantasize their selections of items which could be symbolic of their relationships. Participants could also use paper and crayons to express this exercise if it is impossible to go on a nature walk.

Trainer's Notes: Some members may need special encouragement to be creative and to use fantasy during this exercise.

It may be necessary to distinguish between religiosity and spirituality. Some may tend to see the two as synonymous and have difficulty if they have not ever thought through the differences.

–34–

Wisdom of the Aged

Ajakai Jaya
Glen Jennings

Brief Description: Young couples often lack the resources that could make a difference in their relationships. This exercise helps develop one resource which could make a difference. By pairing older and younger couples, good things often happen.

Objectives:
1. To encourage cross-aged couple relationships.
2. To develop a network of resources for couples.
3. To provide role models for couples to access for improving and maintaining their marital relationships.
4. To provide a vehicle for sharing marital moments that worked.

Materials Needed: None.

Group Composition: Any size group of couples, as evenly split as possible between older couples and younger couples. The ideal would be that the older couples would have strong, healthy marriages and would be at least 20 years older than the younger couples.

Time Required: Thirty to 90 minutes, with the possibility of the exercise becoming an ongoing process for the couples. At times the exercise has been expanded into a half-day exercise.

Rationale: Often couples have few, if any, easily accessed role models for shaping their own marital relationships. Too often younger couples have few resources to turn to in time of need, especially the need to talk and get ideas for improving relationships. This exercise provides two benefits: a role model and someone to turn to in time of need.

Procedures:
1. Identify the younger couples who would be interested in networking with older couples. Then identify the same number of older couples with strong, healthy marriages who would be interested in networking with the younger couples.
2. Younger couples are paired with older couples. In the process, special attention should be given to pairing couples with the possibility of high compatibility.
3. With all couples together, talk briefly about the importance of role models and resources as parts of problem solving, and the benefits that can be reaped from the experiences of couples who have worked through marital problems over time.
4. Instruct the paired couples to find a quiet place where they can talk and share. The older couples are to talk about what it took for them to work through some areas in which the younger couples have questions and concerns.
5. Next, divide everyone into all-female and all-male groups to discuss issues or areas of concern. All group members should review the times when they were more successful in the areas being discussed and what it took to make these things happen. All members should review what each partner did to encourage the success of the other and how each partner encouraged helpfulness from the other.
6. This process can be repeated with cross-gender pairings.
7. This exercise can be concluded with the couples coming together once again, to discuss how hopeful they are about their marriages and about keeping the process going. The older couples are in the position of friends and mentors. Contact can be maintained as desired after the exercise.

Variations: Some groups would benefit from the cross-gender pairings, while it could become problematic for some other groups. For some groups it would be important to keep a wide age differential of at least one generation between the couples.

If it appears that getting communication going could be problematic, the trainer could provide some structure by preparing a list of questions which could be used to get dialogue started. Such a list could include questions about managing money, work and marriage, maintaining spirituality in the marriage, domestic aspects of marriage, togetherness versus separateness, child rearing, maintaining intimacy, couple entertainment, keeping the lines of communication open, etc.

The trainer may want to have the group discuss the benefits and limitations of the pairings becoming an ongoing network which might meet at regular intervals. Some of the pairings may want to establish regular times to meet or to have dinner together.

This exercise can lead to the older couple becoming surrogate grandparents if the younger couple has children. This can be a real asset if the younger couple lives a long distance from their families. Many older couples can get a real sense of passing something on to the next generation by serving as surrogate grandparents. If this develops, the younger couple may need to be cautioned about the possibility of exploiting the situation.

Trainer's Notes: Extreme care should be followed in selecting and pairing the couples together. Sometimes this can be facilitated if the couples are drawn from a common interest pool such as a church, club, or other organization. Couples needing marital therapy should not be admitted to the process.

The trainer may need to discuss the possibility of the process leading to destructive triangles if the talking becomes simply a gripe session about mates. Encourage all talk to be focused on how problems were solved. Also, point out that all relationships have problems and difficult times.

Why Do I Love You?

Stephen Freeman

Brief Description: By reacquainting couples with why they fell in love, the spark can often be rekindled and the fires roar again. Boredom kills more relationships than any other thing. This exercise helps couples to rediscover their love for each other.

Objectives:

1. To allow couples to remember the special things their spouses do (or did) that made them feel special.
2. To allow each person to communicate to the other how special these behaviors or gestures are to him or her.
3. To set a positive tone for the relationship by focusing on some special quality that each person exhibits.
4. To provide a mechanism for helping each person to remember that he or she is special and to remember how often special things are done for him or her.

Materials Needed: Pencil and paper.

Group Composition: This exercise is intended for one couple, but could also be used with groups of couples.

Time Required: Ten to 20 minutes for one couple; increase time proportionately for additional couples.

Rationale: With the passing of the romantic phase, a relationship all too often becomes routine and is accompanied by taking-you-for-granted attitudes. William James expounded that the worst fate that could befall a person is to be ignored. Reaffirming the special things that spouses do for each other and the meaning(s) that attracted them to each other will help to rekindle more rewarding relationships.

Procedures:
1. Provide each couple with paper and pencils and ask them to take five to 10 minutes to list any and all things their spouses do for them which they prize and consider special.
2. Ask the couples to face each other and read (one at a time) their lists and to tell their spouses how these things are special to them.
3. Have the couples exchange lists, with instructions to place them in conspicuous places, such as on the bathroom mirror. Then, each time they do something that is listed as special, they are to put the date beside it.
4. Spouses are to periodically revisit their own lists to visually acknowledge what or how often their spouses do special things for them.
5. The items on the list may be added to or deleted as desired by the owner.

Variations: This exercise can be used with families, or with groups such as a pool of workers. By modifying the exercise to fit the setting and membership, all can become more appreciative of each other.

Another variation is to set a day each week, during which special notes of appreciation are to be written as surprises. This can add a special spark to any relationship, whether intimate or work-related.

Trainer's Notes: This exercise focuses on: acknowledging, rebuilding, and continuing positive aspects of relationships; and on gestures and behaviors that are considered special, regardless of their frequency of occurrence at this time.

The trainer may need to caution participants that this is an exercise which looks only at the positives in relationships, and that it is not a time to get into negatives, or for it to become a gripe session.

SECTION FOUR:
FAMILY/GROUP
DISCUSSION STARTERS

CHAPTER SUMMARIES

Chapter 36. **Backtracking**

This exercise offers a means for family/group members to understand each individual's part in a conflict situation.

Chapter 37. **Teaching Pictures**

The picture cards are designed to be communication starters for family/group members.

Chapter 38. **Rules**

The family/group is given a list of typical rules. The list is used as a discussion starter.

Chapter 39. **Mixer**

This is a building block exercise that uses Legos toys. Blended family members share their feelings with one another in a game format, building upon the Legos base and building stronger relationships.

Chapter 40. **Working Toward a Goal: The Processes**

This exercise is designed to help the group or family to sharpen their skills at goal-setting and accomplishing whatever tasks are necessary to accomplish the goal. The emphasis is on communication, shared responsibilities, and building trust.

Chapter 41.   Blending Together

"The blended family" is given a list of prevalent issues that the family will face. The family uses the questions as a discussion starter.

Chapter 42.   Relationship Myth Deflator Exercise

The family/group is given a list of prevalent relationship myths. The group uses the list as a discussion starter and as a basis for beginning the process for improving relationships.

Chapter 43.   Family/Group Self-Revelation Cards

This fun exercise uses discussion starter cards that stimulate the family/group to engage each member in self-revelation. The cards ask questions that open channels of communication, assisting family/group members in working together in other areas.

Chapter 44.   Sorting Out Priorities

An exercise in which participants go through the process of determining choices, decision making, and sorting out priorities for self versus others.

Chapter 45.   New Traditions

Reconstituted families often need help in establishing new traditions and rituals. This exercise helps them become closer.

Chapter 46.   Wants!

This activity helps the family/group focus on personal and group goals. Members share their personal wants, what they want for the other members, and what they want for the group. After each person shares wants in the three areas, the group discusses the meanings of each person's wants.

Chapter 47.   Promoting Intimacy

This is an activity to get parents involved in the sex education of their children. The activity consists of a set of questions that children of various ages tend to ask parents when the lines of communication are open. Dice are rolled to determine the question and to determine who answers the question.

Chapter 48.   A Moment for Planning

An exercise to help families with the transition that comes with aging and changes in the family structure. Specifically, the exercise is geared toward helping the family at the time a senior member may have to move into a senior living center.

Chapter 49.   Story Writing

This exercise helps the family or group to share feelings in a metaphorical and symbolic way. The result is that the family/group becomes closer.

Chapter 50.   Alternatives Search

This brainstorming exercise helps all to become more flexible in their thinking and more adaptable in their lives. It provides a great opportunity to improve the group's or individual's mental health.

Chapter 51.   What I Meant Was. . .

This exercise is designed to assist participants in clarifying their intentions through understanding of the behaviors (actions) they use to express them.

Chapter 52.   The Hunt

This outdoor exercise is fun and builds a sense of teamwork between couples in the group or pairs in the family. Better relationships and a greater sense of spirituality are promoted by doing this exercise.

36

Backtracking

Ron McManus

Brief Description: This exercise offers a means to understand each individual's part in a conflict situation.

Objectives:
1. To assist members in recognizing their parts in and contributions to conflicts.
2. To be a discussion starter for the participants.

Materials Needed: A copy of the Backtracking Chart for each participant. If the exercise is being used with a family, the chart will need to be enlarged to approximately posterboard size.

Group Composition: Any group with two to 12 members is appropriate.

Time Required: Allow about ten to 20 minutes for recording information, followed by approximately 15 to 30 minutes for discussion.

Rationale: When people understand how their words, actions, and thoughts contribute to difficulties and conflicts, they can begin to work on changing themselves and their situations.

Procedures:
1. The trainer explains that conflict is systematic in that each person plays a part in maintaining it. The trainer then gives an overview of the exercise by explaining that the exercise involves recording your observations of another person, and their recorded observations of you are made known.

2. Ask for volunteers to role-play a family situation, for which about five minutes will be allowed. An example of a situation for five role-players is:

> A mother, father, 17-year-old son, 14-year-old daughter, and eight-year-old daughter are in the living room at home. An argument begins because the 14-year-old daughter is not allowed to go out on "formal dates." The argument is predominately between the father and this daughter.

(A situation should be developed which is relevant for the size and type of group being worked with.)

3. Give a Backtracking Chart to each participant. Ask the role-players to record, in the Words section in the appropriate tracks (columns), the last word they remember speaking before the actual conflict began. Then the role-players record to the best of their recollections their words immediately prior to the ones already written down. This process continues until all role-players have recorded as many of their words that led to the conflict as they can recall. Then explain that the role-players are to continue the process, completing the Actions and Thoughts sections in the same way.

4. Ask the role-players to read over their tracks, then ask them to reflect on how they contributed to the conflict by their words, actions, and thoughts. Encourage them to talk and reflect on what they learned about themselves and relationships from the exercise.

5. Conclude with a few closing comments to the group:
   - This exercise involves reexamining our roles and contributions in relationships.
   - By learning how we contribute to conflicts we can work to correct such disturbances.
   - This exercise gives the participants a tool to aid them in taking control of their own behavior.

Variations: A single Backtracking Chart can be used by the entire family/group, or individual Charts can be provided to each group member. Suggestions for conflict situations that families/groups can role-play are subjects such as: money; child's appearance; helping around the house; discipline; alcohol and drugs; etc.

Trainer's Notes: This exercise is an appropriate assignment for familiar groups such as the family or the business office setting. This exercise can be used with a group that works together to help them see themselves and to add some lighthearted ideas for changes to be made in how they handle conflict in the work area. This exercise can be preceded by a discussion on conflict followed by a discussion in which ideas are shared on ways to reduce conflict and keep it from developing.

BACKTRACKING CHART

CONFLICT SITUATION:_____

_____

	Adult male	Adult female	Adolescent or employee #1	Adolescent or employee #2	Child or employee #3	Child or employee #4
Words What words did you use that caused or contributed to the conflict?						
Actions What actions did you take that caused or contributed to the conflict?						
Thoughts What thoughts did you have that could have caused or contributed to the conflict?						

37

Teaching Pictures

Ron McManus

Brief Description: The picture cards are designed to be communication starters for family/group members.

Objectives:
1. To provide innovative ways of improving relationships.
2. To provide an effective way of examining relationships.
3. To provide a format for discussing family/group issues.

Materials Needed: Provide a set of the 12 concept cards for each participant. A few pieces of construction paper or posterboard should be available for creating new cards.

Group Composition: Small groups or families are most practical for this exercise.

Time Required: Thirty to 45 minutes.

Rationale: The concept cards present simple but important relationship concepts to catch the imagination of the family/group members. The cards are designed to show, tell, and teach group members about their actions. Examples are used that relate to concepts the family/group members can identify with because the concepts come from practical living experiences.

Procedures:
1. Open the exercise with the following comments:
   • Learning is fun.

- Often we learn at unexpected times.
- This exercise centers around presenting simple, ordinary experiences and paralleling these experiences to relationship issues.
- This exercise is designed as more of a "think about this" type of experience.

2. Ask the group to divide into smaller groups of six to ten members each.

3. Explain that the group will receive 12 concept cards. Each card has an illustration and a statement pertaining to the topic. Each group is to examine and discuss the concept cards. Ask the group to think about how the concepts affect their daily living. Allow 15 to 30 minutes for the processing of the cards by each group.

4. Gather everyone back together and open the session for discussion.

5. Conclude by reminding the participants that:
- Lessons that can help bring about change can be positive experiences.
- The concept cards can offer a new way to look at and think about relationship situations.
- The concept cards can be used as homegrowth work.
- New cards can be added by the participants.

Variations: The trainer may provide posterboard to each group and have them create new cards that reflect current issues by using the format of the 12 examples included.

Trainer's Notes: This exercise has many possibilities for use with diverse groups because of the built-in ability of the participants to talk about real issues in a metaphorical way. The trainer can develop cards which are specific to any target group, e.g., office pool, food workers, teachers, parents, adolescents, etc.

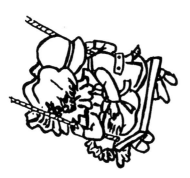

TLC. Sure, TLC usually means "**Tender Loving Care**," but it can also mean "**TRY LOVING CONSTANTLY.**" You will be surprised how situations and attitudes of a family can change if a little fun is inserted into daily living. What better place to insert the fun than with your group/family. Try group/family games, or sharing jokes, or sometimes even allow yourselves to be silly. Every group/family deserves a lot of **TLC–TRY LOVING CONSTANTLY!**

Artwork courtesy of Sharon Jennings.

MAIN-SQUEEZING. A popular expression among young people is to call their boyfriend or girlfriend their main-squeeze. The implication is that these other people are the ones who will show them attention and affection. We need to be able to show our affection with our group/family and be willing to receive and give that wonderful sensation of a squeeze.

Artwork courtesy of Sharon Jennings.

161

DIP-STICKING. A dipstick was always a funny-sounding thing to me. I never really liked the sound of it. The interesting thing is that the name is perfect for what it does. Sometimes others call us names that we do not like to hear. Not always, but sometimes at least, we must realize the names might be appropriate, especially if the name describes exactly what we are doing.

Artwork courtesy of Sharon Jennings.

WRONG-WAY-STREETING. I once heard about a man who rode a bicycle by sitting backwards. People kept telling him he was going the wrong way, but in reality he was going the same way as everyone else, only he was doing it differently. Sometimes children might decide to do things differently from the way we did things. It's easy to say they're headed the wrong way. But if you will take the time to talk to them, you'll often find they're going the same way you went.

Artwork courtesy of Sharon Jennings.

LEAP-FROGGING. It was great fun to play leap-frog as a child. Kids would bend over and others would try to jump over them as if they were not even there. Groups/families sometimes play leap-frog in their relationships. The group/family members jump right over the issues of a problem or crisis instead of trying to work out a solution.

Artwork courtesy of Sharon Jennings.

DOORMATTING. Doormats are made to be stepped on. Doormats are doing their job when they are stepped on and abused with the foot. Groups/families sometimes get confused and think that people are doormats. People are to be loved, not stepped on. Groups/families need to get their thinking straight and realize that if people are treated like doormats, then they are being abused.

Artwork courtesy of Sharon Jennings.

MERRY-GO-ROUNDING. What great fun it is to go to the fair and ride the merry-go-round. It was fun to get on your favorite horse and go around and around and around. For a while this is fun and relaxing, but after a while you usually get tired of going around in a circle. Groups/families sometimes argue about the same issue over and over and over again. They never seem to realize that they are going noplace but in a circle.

Artwork courtesy of Sharon Jennings.

STAR-GAZING. Some people think that if one is good, then one hundred must be better. Well, have you ever looked up at the sky on a clear night and tried to count the stars? There's one, there's two there's three, there's, wait a minute! I already counted that one! It is very easy to lose track of where you are and become confused and give up. Often groups/families think the only way to solve problems is to tackle all the problems at one time. If the group/family would focus on one conflict or problem at a time, they would not be overpowered by the difficulty. Group/family members deserve their own gold stars when they learn how to help the group or family. One way to help is to learn to solve the immediate problem at hand.

Artwork courtesy of Sharon Jennings.

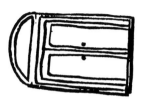

DOOR-BEATING. Think about sitting in your den and suddenly someone starts pounding and beating on your front door. By the time you get out of your chair and get to the front door, you are angry with whomever is knocking so loudly and disturbing you. Some people feel they have to beat on the door, when in reality the doorbell works much better. Group/family members who always try to make a point by being loud or screaming need to learn that if you want to be heard and remembered, **try whispering.**

Artwork courtesy of Sharon Jennings.

SIDE-STEPPING. Have you ever walked down a sidewalk, seen a crack in the concrete and walked around the crack instead of going straight over it? You find yourself side-stepping something you do not want to do. Groups/families often side-step problems they have. The problem might be personality problems, or financial problems, or any of a large number of things. Side-stepping a problem usually only helps in postponing the problem. The problem usually never goes away by doing this.

Artwork courtesy of Sharon Jennings.

FIRE-TRUCKING. When you see a fire truck, what is your natural reaction? Mine is to pull over and get out of its way. When I see the fire truck, I think there is trouble somewhere. Groups/families have their own fire trucks. Groups/families have key words or people that only have to be mentioned or talked about and everyone knows that trouble is near. When groups/families hear their own fire alarms, they usually run away instead of staying around to see if they can help. Remember, only you can prevent relationship fires.

Artwork courtesy of Sharon Jennings.

DIXIE-CUPPING. A dixie-cup dispenser with dixie-cups always sounded like a good idea until I had one. The cups were so small that I kept running out of cups. Some groups/families play the dixie-cup game among themselves. They keep pulling and pulling at each other and they expect the others to keep popping back for more. Well, sometimes the dixie-cup dispenser is **OUT**. Groups/families need to learn that if they continue to pull at others, the only direction the other people can go is **OUT–OUT** the door, **OUT** of their minds, or **OUT** of their lives.

Artwork courtesy of Sharon Jennings.

38

Rules

Ron McManus
Glen Jennings

Brief Description: The family/group is given a list of typical rules. The list is used as a discussion starter.

Objectives:
1. To understand how rules affect the family/group.
2. To clearly understand the family/group's rules.
3. To examine and discuss the family/group's rules.

Materials Needed: A copy of the Rules List for each participant.

Group Composition: Entire families, or small groupings.

Time Required: Approximately 60 to 75 minutes.

Rationale: Rules serve many different purposes for groups and families. Some rules can be helpful to a family or group and some can be harmful. The rules need to be examined from time to time and adjusted as deemed appropriate.

Procedures:
1. Begin by making the following comments to the group:
   - Rules exist everywhere.
   - Rules can be both beneficial and restrictive.
   - Rules that affect relationships need to be continuously re-evaluated.

2. Explain that this exercise is primarily family-oriented. The exercise will be used in this family/group setting to show how the topic can be addressed.
3. Ask the group to divide into smaller groups of three to eight members each.
4. Pass out copies of the Rules List to everyone. Have the groups read over and discuss the list. The group may choose to examine more closely one or more of the rules that concern them.
5. Encourage each group to add any of their own rules to the list.
6. Ask the groups to ask themselves these questions:
   • What are your family/group's rules?
   • How have these rules been helpful or harmful to the family/group?
   • Do any of these rules need to be adjusted?
   • What would happen if some of the rules were changed or eliminated?
   • What will it take to make the rules better for the family/group?
7. Conclude by bringing everyone back together for a brief discussion centered around the question: "What did you learn from the exercise?"

Variations: The family/group may choose to fill out the rules list themselves on the Rules Track sheet. Everyone would first write in the outer track the family/group's existing rules, and then discuss the list. Next, everyone would write in the middle track the undesired family/group rules that exist, and then discuss the list. Lastly, everyone would write in the inner track the desired rules for their family/group, and then discuss them. The Rules Track can be enlarged to posterboard size so that the responses can be recorded and later displayed to help the family/group as they work to establish new rules and relationships.

Trainer's Notes: The trainer needs to give special attention to the adjustments that may be required, depending upon the level of the participants' negotiation skills, and upon the nature of the family/group, e.g., blended family, adoptive family, abusive family, emotionally close group, emotionally distant group, etc.

RULES LIST

- Children are to be seen, not heard!

- Never talk back to your parents.

- Bedtime for all children is 9:00 p.m.

- All phone calls are limited to *five minutes*.

- Never cry in public.

- "No wife of mine will ever work as long as I can support my family!"

- In this family/group obedience is more valued than relationships.

- Parents deserve respect simply because they are parents.

- Tenderness is weakness.

- The way you behave is more important that the way you really are.

- Strong feelings are harmful.

- Rules should never be broken.

- The boss is always right.

- Never question the company's policies.

- What a person knows is more important than how he or she feels.

- The company is always more important than an individual.

- Seniority must always dictate to youth.

- Father always knows best.

- Obedience makes a child strong.

- Toughness with children makes for strong adults.

- Kindness is the way to spoil a child.

- Professionalism is more important than kindness with patients.

- Homework is always to be done before you eat.

- Refunds are never made without a cash receipt.

- Anger is never tolerated in this house.

- Always squeeze the toothpaste from the bottom of the tube.

- Children never know better than adults.

- Children never can be trusted.

- A high degree of self-esteem in children will lead to trouble as adults.

- Children should always love their parents.

- Work is more important in this family than living or having fun.

- Giving children freedom will ruin them as adults.

- The group is never as important as the individual's freedom.

- The customer is always right.

RULES TRACK

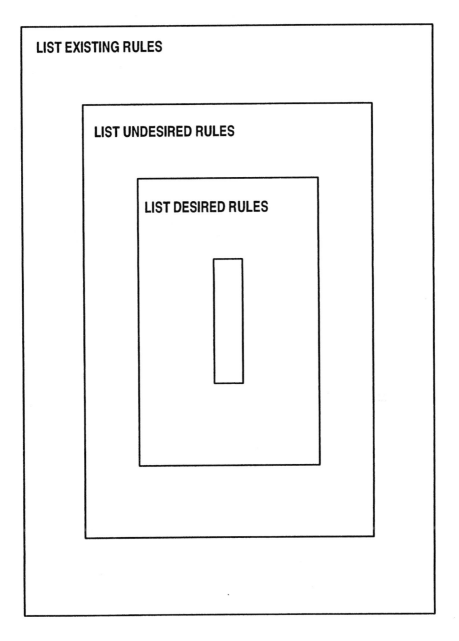

LIST EXISTING RULES

LIST UNDESIRED RULES

LIST DESIRED RULES

39

Mixer

Sherrie Moore
Ron McManus

Brief Description: This is a building block exercise that uses Legos toys. Blended family members share their feelings with one another in a game format, building upon the Legos base and building stronger relationships.

Objectives:
1. To encourage more open communication within the blended family.
2. To identify problem areas in a relationship system.
3. To evaluate feelings of belonging to a unit.

Materials Needed: Legos (toy building set, green base), dice, and game cards.

Group Composition: Small group or family units (three to five members).

Time Required: Thirty to 45 minutes.

Rationale: People in new relationships need fun times to learn more about one another. Often members of new relationships have difficulty breaking the silence and getting into a self-revealing mode of interaction. This game facilitates communication in a very pleasant and fun way.

Procedures:

1. Open the exercise with the following comments:
   - Learning how and what to communicate in a new relationship can be difficult.
   - Structured exercises that encourage communication can benefit new relationships.
   - This exercise uses a game format to help individuals get to know one another.
2. Ask for three to five volunteers to play and demonstrate the game.
3. The players are seated around a table and each is given an equal number of Legos pieces to begin the game. Each rolls the dice to determine the largest number, then the player with the largest number plays first.
4. The player who is to start first draws a card, reads it aloud, and responds to the card. If two or more of the other players agree that the response is appropriate, the player gets to place a Legos piece on the base. If less than two players indicate the response is appropriate, the player does not get to place a Legos piece on the base. Play moves to the next player.
5. The next player draws a card and responds to it, then the other players evaluate it as appropriate or inappropriate.
6. Play continues until one player has his or her base covered. This player is the winner.

Variations: This exercise can be made more meaningful and timely if players will make cards specific to their family/group situation. By making cards specific to their relationships, the players are more likely to improve their relationships and play the game more often.

Trainer's Notes: Although this exercise was originated to be used with blended families, it can quite easily be adapted to be used with any new group such as merged departments, merged work units, new neighbors, at the beginning of a school year, or other times in which new groups are formed.

GAME CARD QUESTIONS

What is your favorite memory?

Tell what you like about your new family/group.

What do you miss most from your former family/group?

What is your favorite leisure time activity?

I wish I could _____ .

One of my most memorable times was _____ .

This new family/group is _____ .

Tell about one of your most frightening experiences.

I feel appreciated when _____ .

I wish I were less _____ .

I feel most loved _____ .

I wish this family/group would _____ .

One of the things I like about _____ is _____ .

Tell about one of your greatest concerns for this new family/group.

Compare this family/group to a musical instrument.

Tell about a time you were emotionally hurt.

I will feel accepted and a part of this family/group when _____ .

Working Toward a Goal: The Processes

Laura McLachlin

Brief Description: This exercise is designed to help the group or family to sharpen their skills at goal-setting and accomplishing whatever tasks are necessary to accomplish the goal. The emphasis is on communication, shared responsibilities, and building trust.

Objectives:
1. To promote group strength and cohesion.
2. To facilitate discussion and group processes.
3. To provide an opportunity to express feelings about the group and the group processes.

Materials Needed: A watch, and a rope or some other thing to use as a barrier.

Group Composition: A group consisting of six to ten people. Members can be individuals who are coming together for the first time, or who have know each other for an extended period of time, such as a family.

Time Required: Ten to 15 minutes for the activity. Another 15 to 45 minutes should be allotted for processing and discussing the exercise.

Rationale: Membership within a group (work, family, church, etc.) typically requires working toward a goal. In functional groups, all members work together to accomplish the common goal. When working toward a common goal, responsibilities must be shared. This distribution of duties often creates feelings of anxiety, anger, fear, etc. This exercise is designed to (a) explore participants' feelings when given a task to accomplish, (b) build trust among group members, and (c) enhance communication among individuals.

Procedures:
1. One end of the rope should be secured to a stable object. The other end should be held by the trainer. The rope should be held at about four feet from the floor.
2. Begin the exercise by telling the group a life threatening scenario. (Example: You are on a wilderness expedition together and have suddenly walked into a large pit of quicksand. The only escape is to climb onto a nearby branch.)
3. Emphasis should be placed on *safety* and survival of all group members.
4. Instruct the group members that they have only two minutes to discuss a plan of how they will get the group over the rope. They are to use only themselves. No props are allowed.
5. Following the two-minute planning session, the group must remain silent throughout the rest of the exercise. Instruct the group that they have ten minutes to complete the task.

Variations: Participants can be allowed to verbally communicate throughout the entire exercise. Another variation allows only one person (designated by the group) to speak after the two minute planning session while the other group members remain silent.

Time should be adjusted according to each group's needs and number of participants.

The focus of this exercise is not on accomplishing the task; focus should be on the process the group experiences to work toward the goal.

Trainer's Notes: This is a valuable diagnostic exercise to identify roles within a group. The trainer should be silent during the exercise and speak only when safety precautions need to be enforced.

It is important for the trainer to remain supportive and accepting toward the group or family. Judgments should not be made if the group is unable to complete the task–the important thing is for the group to talk about their feelings, thoughts, etc. and to fully process the experience.

Discussion should focus on participants' feelings during the exercise, how they felt toward other group members, what they would do differently, etc. Further discussion may include how the outcome of this exercise relates to other group goals.

41

Blending Together

Ron McManus

Brief Description: "The blended family" is given a list of prevalent issues that the family will face. The family uses the questions as a discussion starter.

Objectives:
1. To recognize some of the problems encountered by blended family members.
2. To develop a basis for understanding the problems and each other.
3. To open dialogue which facilitates adjustment.

Materials Needed: A copy of the Blended Family Issues list for each participant.

Group Composition: The blended family.

Time Required: Forty-five to 60 minutes.

Rationale: "Blended family" is a relatively new term. A blended family is exactly what it sounds like–members from two different families that blend together by living together to become one family. As a new family, the blended family members encounter very new problems. This exercise offers an experience for understanding and communicating among family members.

Procedures:
1. Open with the following comments:
   • Divorce affects each family member differently.

- Many new marriages bring together members with very different pasts who will be developing relationships.
- Finding ways so that everybody feels like they fit into the new relationship system can often be very difficult.
- This exercise examines how people can "blend" into new relationships.

2. Explain that this exercise is primarily family relationship-oriented. The exercise will be used in this setting to show how the topic can be addressed.

3. Pass out a copy of the Blended Family Issues list to everyone, and have group members read over and discuss the list. The group may choose to examine more closely one or more of the issues.

4. Encourage each group to add to the list any issues that they deem appropriate.

5. Bring everyone back together and asks for a report from each group. The report should center around:
   - What did you learn from the exercise?
   - Was the exercise beneficial? How?
   - What are some of the creative solutions thought of for the issue?
   - What new issues should be added to the list?

6. Conclude the session with an open discussion.

Variations: The family may choose to add to the Blended Family Issues list after they have discussed it. The family discusses each of the issues of concern and asks themselves these questions:
- How has the issue affected us?
- Why have we allowed the issue to continue?
- What will it take to correct the issue?

Trainer's Notes: This is an excellent exercise developed and refined for use with blended families. It can be useful in training others to be sensitive to more of the issues faced by blended families. It points out the importance for anyone who works with blended families or children from blended families to have empathy for some of the family's issues.

BLENDED FAMILY ISSUES

- What do I call my parent's new mate?
- Do I have to have the new parent's permission to do what I want to do?
- Will all children be treated equally?

- Is it all right to grieve over the loss of my original family?
- Why do I have to share my mom/dad with all these people?
- What role will my other birth parent have in my life now?

- Can I love my new parent?
- Am I disloyal if I continue to want to see my other birth parent?
- How should blended grandparents be related to?

- What would I like for my new parent to call me?
- What will it take for this new family to make it?
- How do I communicate with two families?

42

Relationship Myth Deflator Exercise

Ron McManus
Glen Jennings

Brief Description: The family/group is given a list of prevalent relationship myths. The group uses the list as a discussion starter and as a basis for beginning the process for improving relationships.

Objectives:
    1. To understand that there are relationship myths.
    2. To examine and discuss relationship needs.

Materials Needed: A copy of the Relationship Myths List for each participant, and a balloon.

Group Composition: A group or family of any number who are interested in looking at relationships.

Time Required: Forty-five to 60 minutes.

Rationale: Myths are fables, legends, or partial truths embodying the convictions of a person or group. Myths have been upheld and unchallenged for so long that they now appear to be factual events or occurrences. Most myths originate from a one-time occurrence or from a partial truth that has been generalized beyond its circumstances. Myths often prevent people from achieving their full potential in relationships.

    Every area of human endeavor has its own mythology which limits human productivity and robs people of greater satisfaction.

Often people are so busy chasing the myths or testing relationships that they have unrealistic expectations for the relationship or environment (workplace).

Procedures:
1. Begin the session by blowing up a balloon and making the following comments:
   A. I have three options of things I can do with this balloon:
      • I can tie a knot in the end of the balloon and it will stay enlarged.
      • I can let the balloon go and watch it jet across the room.
      • I can burst the balloon with a sharp instrument.
   B. I want you to keep these options in mind as we start this exercise.
   C. This exercise pertains to myths that affect relationships. The exercise will give you an opportunity to see how myths can affect our relationships. Some of the myths may be relevant to some of your relationships.
2. Ask the group to divide into smaller groups of three to six members each.
3. Pass out a copy of the Relationship Myth List to each participant. Have the groups read the list and discuss the myths. The groups may choose to more closely examine one or more of the myths.
4. Encourage each group to add any myths that they are aware of.
5. Asks the groups to ask themselves these questions:
   • What is the myth? What is the truth?
   • How has the myth been helpful or harmful?
   • Why has the myth been allowed to persist?
   • What will it take to correct the myth?
6. Conclude by bringing everyone back to the original large group for a brief discussion of the exercise. The session may be opened to anyone who wants to talk or the trainer may center the discussion around the following questions:
   • What did the exercise mean?
   • Was the exercise beneficial? In what way?
   • How will the exercise help you in your relationships?
   • What myths would you add to the list?

Variations: This exercise can be adapted for use with groups of different kinds, e.g., personnel workers, office pools, teachers, adolescents, nurses, teachers, auto mechanics, ministers, nursing home care workers, custodians, etc. Every area of life has its own myths and half-truths which can be examined in this format.

This exercise can be made more meaningful by having each participant select a myth to write on a balloon. Write the myth on the balloon, blow it up, and then pop it, thus exploding the myth. They could also let the balloon fly away as if the myth was jetting out of their life.

Trainer's Notes: Some people are rather reluctant to give up their myths. Probably the more often they have espoused the myths with others, the more difficulty they will have in letting go of the myth and dealing with the truth. It may help participants if the trainer can share an experience in which it was difficult to admit something he or she believed was a myth.

RELATIONSHIP MYTH LIST

- Marriage should always be a happy state.
- In good relationships people never want to be apart.
- There should never be anything withheld in a relationship.
- Marital partners should always agree with each other.
- The other person's needs should always come first.
- "And they lived happily ever after."
- For a good relationship, partners should always see eye-to-eye.
- Opposites are always more compatible.
- There must be equal give-and-take in a relationship.
- Continual testing of a relationship is the best way to know the quality of the relationship.
- One should always feel closer to one's mate than to anyone else.
- A good relationship never seems to have a need to change.
- In an argument, someone is right and someone is wrong.
- Relationships should never require work, otherwise they shouldn't have been.
- Keeping serious is the best way to maintain a relationship.
- Never admit a weakness or let the other see you cry.
- Good relationships do not require forgiveness on anyone's part.
- More sex makes all relationships better.
- Good friends can never be lovers.

Family/Group Self-Revelation Cards

Ron McManus
Glen Jennings

Brief Description: This fun exercise uses discussion starter cards that stimulate the family/group to engage each member in self-revelation. The cards ask questions that open channels of communication, assisting family/group members in working together in other areas.

Objectives:
1. To provide a vehicle for self-revelation and for increasing communication.
2. To offer an opportunity for gaining insight which will lead to improved relationships.

Materials Needed: Make one set of 3 × 5 Family/Group Self-Revelation Cards for each group.

Group Composition: Small groups of four to ten members each.

Time Required: Thirty to 60 minutes.

Rationale: One of the most difficult things for group members to do is to share information about themselves. When sharing occurs in a fun setting, the experience offers all participants many rewards.

Procedures:
1. Explain that this exercise is a way for individuals to get better acquainted. The group is divided into small groups of four to ten members each.

2. Provide each group with a set of Family/Group Self-Revelation Cards.

3. Suggest that each group select someone to be the first card selector. This person selects the top card from the deck and responds to the card, then places the card at the bottom of the deck.

4. Play continues around the group in a clockwise manner until time to quit is called.

5. Call the large group back together. Ask them to respond to the following questions:
   - How will this exercise help this group in the work environment?
   - What did you learn about yourself?
   - Who do you appreciate more now than you did before this activity began?
   - Who would you like to know better?
   - How may this improve your relationship with someone in the group?

6. Conclude the exercise by stating that relationships are based upon and nourished by communication between individuals. Learning to communicate more openly with others can be fun and informative.

Variations: The exercise can be used with family groups, especially extended families and at family gatherings such as reunions. Groups and families should be encouraged to make their own cards.

Trainer's Notes: If the group members are basically total strangers to each other, the trainer may want to do some self-revelation when introducing the exercise. This can be very freeing for the group and enhance the effectiveness of the exercise.

With some groups the trainer may want to have an easel or chalkboard for recording some of the responses to the questions. This helps participants to see and be more aware of the benefits of the exercise. This can be a nice way to bring closure.

FAMILY/GROUP SELF-REVELATION CARDS

- Tell about the first time you used a machine.
- Introduce yourself as your mother would introduce you to this group.
- Describe your favorite dessert.
- Share one of your most embarrassing moments.
- Tell how you are most like your mother.
- Introduce yourself as your father would introduce you to this group.
- Tell about your first day on the job with your present employer.
- Tell about your first job.
- Share one of your most common fantasies.
- How are you most like your immediate supervisor?
- What song or book reminds you of the company you work for at present?
- How is your current job better than your previous job?
- How are you most like your father?
- Share one of your most proud moments.
- What concerns you the most about aging?
- What qualities do you like in a friend?
- Tell about one of your most touching moments.
- What value do you wish all people would live by?
- How much personal space is most comfortable for you?
- Tell the name of your all-time favorite movie and why it is your favorite.
- What qualities do you respect in a boss or supervisor?
- Describe someone you have much respect for. Do not give his or her name.
- What do you like best about yourself?
- Share one of your most frightening moments.
- If you could go anywhere for a two-week vacation, where would you go and why?
- Share one of your greatest challenges.
- What song best describes or symbolizes the family you grew up in? Why?
- What would you like for your life to be like in 20 years?
- What is your favorite food? Why?

- What do you value most from your youth?
- What is your favorite leisure time activity?
- How are you most like a grandparent of yours?
- What are you feeling at this time about this exercise?

44

Sorting Out Priorities

Laura McLachlin

Brief Description: An exercise in which participants go through the process of determining choices, decision-making, and sorting out priorities for self versus others.

Objectives:
1. To improve awareness of influences of others on decision making.
2. To increase problem-solving and decision-making skills and abilities.
3. To increase awareness of personal needs and choices in life.

Materials Needed: Sorting Out Priorities form and pencils.

Group Composition: Individual, small group, or a family.

Time Required: Thirty to 75 minutes.

Rationale: Understanding how external forces (societal, family, peer, and others) influence people is important to increasing awareness of personal needs, and to decision making and problem solving. Through this exercise, participants can develop a better understanding of how outside influences affect their personal lives.

Procedures:
1. Hand out a Sorting Out Priorities form and a pencil to each individual. Instruct each person to complete the sentences as they apply to him/her. Allow ten to 15 minutes for completion.

2. Discussion may center around how others influence choices, taking responsibility for decision making, differences between decisions made by others and by the participants on their own behalf, societal expectations of behaviors, barriers to self-expression, dependencies, etc.

Variations: The trainer may want to change the title of the exercise according to the time of year, the theme desired, or the composition of the family/group. The trainer may want to change some or all of the sentence stems on the Sorting Out Priorities form to accentuate areas for exploration.

Trainer's Notes: The trainer should approach this exercise with care and support toward participants as some of the issues may be difficult to discuss.

SORTING OUT PRIORITIES

Complete each sentence as quickly as possible. Most likely the first thoughts are the best ones to jot down in the space provided.

1. My parents would like me to _____

   _____

2. My mate would like me to _____

   _____

3. My children (if no children think of someone to put in place of

   children) would like me to _____

   _____

4. My friends would like me to _____

   _____

5. My doctor would like me to _____

   _____

6. My therapist would like me to _____

   _____

7. My co-workers would like me to _____

_____

8. I would like to _____

_____

_____

_____

45

New Traditions

Ajakai Jaya
Glen Jennings

Brief Description: Reconstituted families often need help in establishing new traditions and rituals. This exercise helps them become closer.

Objectives:
1. To lighten holiday tensions.
2. To provide a tradition or ritual that fosters a sense of connectedness.
3. To build a history of specialness which can help the family to move through difficult times.

Materials Needed: None specifically. Depending upon the tradition to be developed, members may need to secure specific props and materials.

Group Composition: One or more reconstituted families. The exercise may need to be limited to a specific number of families as too many families may make for awkwardness.

Time Required: The time line for this exercise will vary tremendously depending upon the traditions to be developed and the number of families involved. With one family, the time required for the exercise may be rather short. Most likely the tradition or ritual will be more powerful if it is an appropriate time capsule and in an air of seriousness. The exercise can be limited to 30 to 60 minutes in terms of setting up the tradition. The actual carrying out of the tradition can be done outside of the group setting when the families may have more time.

Rationale: Traditions and rituals can either strengthen relationships or become a drag on relationships. Reconstituted families often have too little sense of connectedness and can be strengthened by developing their own "new" traditions. Traditions and rituals often serve as anchors in the storms of life; this exercise can be quite beneficial in helping people to feel grounded and connected.

Procedures:
1. Begin by having the members of the family or families discuss the part of the holiday season that is most meaningful to each. They may need to discuss what from their past they would like to continue in terms of family celebrations.
2. Then the family or families should discuss what they would like to be different in the future.
3. Encourage the family to think creatively about the type of traditions or rituals they would like to establish in the reconstituted family. Encourage them to think of the ritual as an opportunity to foster a new stage in the life of the family. This new tradition should be easily repeated and should also be something the members will want to do in the coming years.
4. The family will need to make some rather detailed plans for implementing the new tradition. The planning stage should provide an air of expectation for becoming closer and more intimate.
5. Have the family or families implement their "new tradition."

Variations: The family may want to talk with other families about traditions and their values before beginning this exercise. Although most traditions are centered around holidays and special times (birthdays, births, anniversaries, etc.), many families have found it beneficial to create their own traditions which are not tied to holidays.

Too often families get stuck thinking that traditions are expensive; this need not be the case. Encourage the family to think in terms of nonexpensive traditions that are simple yet powerful.

Trainer's Notes: The trainer may want to develop a list of traditions which other families have found to be helpful to them. Some families will need special encouragement to think creatively. By thinking creatively the family may avoid the pain of traditions from their previous families.

Traditions often get families in touch with the loss of members. This can be difficult for some families; thus, the trainer may need to help the family to use the loss as a time to grow stronger.

46

Wants!

Glen Jennings

Brief Description: This activity helps the family/group focus on personal and group goals. Members share their personal wants, what they want for the other members, and what they want for the group. After each person shares wants in the three areas, the group discusses the meanings of each person's wants.

Objectives:
1. To assist individuals and the group to establish personal and group goals.
2. To provide a model for assertiveness of personal goals.
3. To teach a more democratic interaction method for future use by the family/group.

Materials Needed: Pens and paper for each participant; a flip chart and marker for recording "wants" as they are shared.

Group Composition: Small family-size groups of four to eight members.

Time Required: Forty-five to 75 minutes, depending upon the number of groups formed.

Rationale: Many groups and families seem to be adrift in the sea of life; this exercise helps such groups establish some direction and commitment to each other. Within some groups there is little opportunity for all to assert their wants. This exercise will assist even the most timid and quietest to be heard.

Procedures:
1. Explain the importance of goals:
   • Goals give direction to life.
   • Fulfillment of goals provides greater life satisfaction.
   • By understanding others' goals, we have a better understanding of others and how to help them.
2. Point out the importance of being able to identify and state goals in a meaningful, assertive manner.
3. Instruct all to list the following three headings an equal distance apart on their papers:
   • I WANT FOR ME...........
   • I WANT FOR YOU.........
   • I WANT FOR THIS FAMILY/GROUP..........
4. Allow 10-20 minutes for members to write their wants.
5. Beginning with the youngest member, ask all members in turn to share their list of wants.
6. Record on the flip chart the wants identified as each member shares his/her list with the group. Put the members' initials by their wants. (This may be useful later.)
7. Lead the group in clarifying the meaning of each member's wants.
8. Ask each member what would happen if members committed themselves to helping fulfill these goals.
9. Ask what would happen if each member were to achieve his/her personal wants.
10. Now direct each family or group in converting their flip chart into a poster which they can display in their home or work place (group).
11. Bring closure to the group by reviewing the importance of goals and discussing the commitment required to achieve goals.

Variations: This exercise is especially powerful and meaningful when used with a family. The more traditional the family the more meaningful, as every member learns how to be assertive about his or her wants. This can be very helpful with families in which one member exerts undue control over the family.

For families with few boundaries, it is often beneficial to help them refine the original goals to a few well-defined and achievable goals.

Trainer's Notes: If the group or family has young children who are unable to write their wants, the trainer should sit next to the child and write the wants the child dictates.

For families with multiple problems, this exercise should come near the end of therapy. Less dysfunctional families and healthy families can enter early on into such an exercise.

It often benefits the family to exaggerate the results that could be achieved when all commit to these goals.

Promoting Intimacy

Glen Jennings

Brief Description: This is an activity to get parents involved in the sex education of their children. The activity consists of a set of questions that children of various ages tend to ask parents when the lines of communication are open. Dice are rolled to determine the question and to determine who answers the question.

Objectives:
1. To open the barrier to formal sex education.
2. To educate children about some of the basics of sexuality.
3. To provide a set of appropriate questions for beginning the process of sex education.
4. To assist parents in becoming more involved in the formal sex education of their children.

Materials Needed: The Sex Talk Questions (in card form) and a set of courageous parents.

Group Composition: The family or other close group.

Time Required: Thirty to 60 minutes.

Rationale: All children need to learn about love, affection, intimacy, sexuality, sex, reproduction, contraception, parenting, and relationship responsibility. Many parents would like for their children to learn about these topics but lack the support necessary to do the job. This exercise, whether done under the guidance of the counselor or simply by parents, is most likely to begin a process which will continue throughout life. This exercise often lays down a foundation which is the basis for enriching the parent-child relationship over their lifetimes.

Procedures:
1. Begin by stating that this exercise is a preparation for how adults can address the issue of human sexuality with children. Discuss the activity with the parents in advance of mentioning it in front of the children. At this time it is important to support the parents and show empathy for their concern for entering into such a sensitive area with their children.
2. Give the parents a set of The Sex Talk Questions cards at least one week in advance of beginning the activity. Encourage the parents to set aside some time for just the two of them to review and practice with the cards. *Do not spring the cards on the parents in an unexpected way or time.*
3. Commend the parents and family for being willing to begin such an important journey. Assure them that the rewards will be worth the time and effort required.
4. Have the family sit in a circle on the floor or in soft chairs.
5. Ask the youngest child to roll the dice; if an even number comes up, the mother answers the question (the top card of the deck) and if an odd number comes up, the father answers the question.
6. After the appropriate parent answers the question to the best of his/her ability, play moves to the next older child. Play continues in this manner until the oldest child has rolled the dice and the card has been answered. Then the mother and father each take a turn rolling the dice and having the card answered. Next play returns to the youngest child and continues as long as the trainer determines (usually 30 to 60 minutes).
7. Bring closure to the activity by asking the family what feelings they had while playing the cards. It may be beneficial to self-reveal something about your own sex education or some experience about doing such an activity with your family. Also say a few words about quality sex education being intended to enrich family life, to foster intimacy rather than sex, to prepare

people for long-lasting and caring relationships, and to reduce exploitation of others.

Variations: Many families could be enriched by involving the grandparents in this exercise. Some families may want to add their own questions to the list provided. For precocious families, the whole family can take turns in answering the questions.

Trainer's Notes: The trainer should go over the set of questions with the parents in advance of the sessions in which children participate. Much of the success of the exercise is likely to depend upon the sense of support the parents receive from the counselor. Some parents would definitely benefit from reviewing a good book on human sexuality before undertaking this exercise.

The trainer may want to have a bibliography of sex education books to provide to parents for their reference use. The list should identify books appropriate for different aged children and some appropriate for adults.

The trainer should key in on the parents' value system and respect it at all times. Also, it is quite helpful to use terms such as "appropriate" and "inappropriate" rather than "good," "bad," "right," or "wrong" when doing sex education.

It is crucial that the trainer/counselor be somewhat comfortable with his or her own sexuality before becoming involved in sex education. At the same time it is best to share with parents that it is not necessary for them to be totally comfortable with their own sexuality and with the topic of sex education before undertaking family sex education. If parents are told that they should be totally comfortable with the topic before beginning family sex education, they will never begin doing sex education, because few people are ever totally comfortable with the topic–not even the experts.

THE SEX TALK QUESTIONS

1. What is love?

2. Where do babies come from?

3. Why can't Daddies have babies?

4. Is sex fun?

5. What is sexual responsibility?

6. Why do boys have penises and girls vaginas?

7. How do babies get out of mothers?

8. What is orgasm?

9. What are wet dreams?

10. How do babies get in the mother?

11. How are twins made?

12. How old should a person be before beginning sex?

13. What is a tampon?

14. What is VD (venereal diseases)? What are STDs (sexually transmitted diseases)?

15. What is a rubber?

16. Why are some boys circumcised? What is circumcision?

17. Why do some girls get pregnant so young?

18. Why do boys like to look at girls' breasts?

19. What is homosexual?

20. Does sex hurt?

21. Why do parents want their children to wait to have sex?

22. What is rape?

23. What is masturbation? How do girls masturbate?

24. Is it OK to masturbate?

25. When should a person begin to have sex?

26. What is the clitoris?

27. Why do boys have balls?

28. What are ovaries?

29. What is a hermaphrodite?

30. Why do some people call others dirty names?

31. What is a whore? Can a whore be either male or female?

32. Can a person be over-sexed?

33. Do women like sex? Do all men like sex?

34. When is it OK to kiss and hold hands?

35. What is French kissing?

36. How will a person know when they are ready to have sex?

37. Why do some adults want to have sex with children?

38. Do people have to be married to have sex?

39. What is oral sex?

40. How should people prevent pregnancy?

41. What is incest?

42. What does it take to be a good parent?

43. How does the pill prevent pregnancy?

44. Do old people have sex? Do they enjoy it?

45. Why do females menstruate? What is it?

A Moment for Planning

Ajakai Jaya

Brief Description: An exercise to help families with the transition that comes with aging and changes in the family structure. Specifically, the exercise is geared toward helping the family at the time a senior member may have to move into a senior living center.

Objectives:
1. To help families adapt to changes in the family structure due to aging of one of its members.
2. To provide adequate input from the senior family member.
3. To lay the groundwork for maintaining good relationships into the future.

Materials Needed: None; however, a comfortable seating arrangement enhances the exercise. Ideally all should be sitting in a circle so each can see each other. At times a chalkboard or flip chart may facilitate the exercise, especially the decision-making process. The flip chart can be used to record the major concerns as they are mentioned.

Group Composition: All family members should be invited to the exercise. The senior person must be included.

Time Required: One to two hours is usually an adequate time.

Rationale: When decisions are made which involve a member's life and living situation it is crucial that the member be present. When people have input to decisions they are more likely to support that decision. This is especially true when it involves the discussion about placing a senior family member in a different living situation.

Procedures:
1. Discuss with the senior person who he/she wants at the family meeting. Honor his/her requests by trying to get those people to attend and try to limit any who are not wanted at the meeting.
2. Designate one family member to keep accurate notes of the meeting. It might be wise to tape record the meeting for later reference.
3. Begin with the senior person expressing his/her wishes.
4. Encourage others to express their concerns.
5. List the major concerns on the flip chart.
6. Return to the senior person for feedback. Give special attention to what he/she sees as necessities and other things which will foster his/her sense of comfort, safety, and security.
7. Negotiate a decision which the senior can be comfortable with.
8. Finally, the senior is asked to leave a word of wisdom with the family. This is a time for the senior to be considered by loved ones as a person in control and of elevated status. It is also a time to specify desires and to assign tasks. This eliminates the probability that one person will do all the caretaking of the eldest member of the family. It will also foster better relationships in the future.

Variations: The leader may want to preface all of this by encouraging the senior person to do some research on senior centers and the advantages and disadvantages of transition options. The leader may want to encourage the senior person to talk with others who have made transitions of this nature.

Trainer's Notes: This situation needs to be handled with extreme sensitivity to the senior's needs, expectations, wants, and values. The trainer may want to develop materials to place in the family's hands in preparation for the meeting.

49

Story Writing

Stephen Freeman

Brief Description: This exercise helps the family or group to share feelings in a metaphorical and symbolic way. The result is that the family/group becomes closer.

Objectives:
1. To develop more skill in talking and sharing feelings.
2. To help group members form closer relationships.
3. To provide practice incorporating thoughts and feelings into congruent behavior.

Materials Needed: Chalkboard and chalk or newsprint and markers for recording comments.

Group Composition: Small group or family.

Time Required: Thirty to 60 minutes.

Rationale: Some people have difficulty recognizing and labeling a feeling. This exercise provides an opportunity for emotional identification and sharing of feelings. The story can act as a springboard to talk about feelings, values, and goals. Stories can facilitate self-exploration. The relationship of the feeling evoked by the story can provide self-understanding for group members.

Procedures:
1. Introduce the exercise with the following remarks:
    a. Feelings are neither good nor bad. They just are!

    b. Awareness of one's feelings is healthy and freeing.

    c. Feelings are normal. Not all feelings need to be expressed. Once one is aware of a feeling, a choice can be made whether or not to express it.

2. Explain that this exercise is designed to illicit emotional identification and subsequently lead to defining needs and goals in a nonthreatening atmosphere.

3. Explain that the stories will provide a springboard for discussion and provide an opportunity for self-exploration and awareness.

4. Each group/family member is invited to contribute one or more lines to the story. The trainer helps the group/family develop a particular theme to the story and offers words such as "and," "moreover," "then," "however" in order to keep the story flowing. Assist members to be creative by helping them utilize their senses and imagination.

5. Initially, the group may need to be primed by giving them sentence stems. Some suggestions are: "If you really knew me . . . " "When I feel lonely . . . " "I smile whenever . . . " "Happiness is . . . " "The key to my door . . . " "I can't seem to forget . . . " "Over and over again . . . "

6. Someone in the group begins the story and others contribute until the theme is developed and a conclusion is reached.

7. Next, lead a brief discussion about the feelings, goals, and values that were expressed.

8. To conclude the session, congratulate the participants for the risks that were taken.

Variations: Participants may choose to draw a picture to depict their story and have others add to it. Also, a member may choose to sculpt the story.

Trainer's Notes: The trainer needs to be cautious of intellectualization or evoking feelings that members may not be prepared to handle.

50

Alternatives Search

Laura McLachlin

Brief Description: This brainstorming exercise helps all to become more flexible in their thinking and more adaptable in their lives. It provides a great opportunity to improve the group's or individual's mental health.

Objectives:
1. To improve problem-solving and decision-making skills.
2. To promote group interaction and cohesion.

Materials Needed: Slips of paper and a "hat," or chalkboard and chalk; plain paper and pencils.

Group Composition: Individual, small group, or family.

Time Required: Forty-five to 90 minutes depending upon number in group or family.

Rationale: The process of brainstorming within a group can be an exciting experience. It can provide refreshing ideas, different thoughts, and creative solutions to problems.

Procedures:
1. Divide the large group into smaller groups of two to four people, or individuals may work alone. Either have groups draw statements from a hat or select from a list on chalkboard:
   a. Things to do on a weekend in this town.
   b. Things to do by myself.

    c. Ways to make friends.

    d. Ways to make work/school fun.

    e. Things to do without spending a cent.

    f. Things to do on a Monday night.

    g. Things to do with one other person.

    h. Things to do with your family.

    i. Things to do when feeling depressed.

    j. Things to do within walking distance of here.

2. After the brainstorming session, the groups, families, or individuals should rank order the list and select the top three for each item. These three alternatives will be presented to the group.

3. Discussion involves alternatives selected, the process of selection (any problems, how were the top three selected, etc.), and how this process is used in everyday life to select activities, etc.

Variations: Situations may be changed to meet group, family, and/or individual needs and interests.

Trainer's Notes: Maintain the flow of discussion by asking questions. Discussion can also focus on group processes. Group members can learn how they go about solving problems and creating ideas.

–51–

What I Meant Was . . .

Stephen Freeman

Brief Description: This exercise is designed to assist participants in clarifying their intentions through understanding of the behaviors (actions) they use to express them.

Objectives:
1. To help participants understand that intentions have a powerful effect on our actions.
2. To help participants to learn how changing actions usually means changing intentions.
3. To help participants to not analyze their intentions but rather believe their actions, since conflicting intentions can result in conflicting behaviors.

Materials Needed: None. Specific feedback about behavior (past, current, or future) is the goal of the exercise.

Group Composition: This exercise can be used quite easily with couples, families, or other groups.

Time Required: For couples or small families, this exercise can be done in 30-60 minutes. Larger groups will require more time.

Rationale: Intentions are often unclear, at least consciously. Consistently analyzing our intentions leads more to intellectualizing than to any real changing. Being aware of our true intentions, plus making commitments to future actions, can demonstrate that we do live up to our commitments, and builds up trust in relationships.

Procedures:

1. This exercise may be introduced by saying, as if to a prospective date, "Sir, what are your intentions toward my daughter?" or "Mary, you don't want to go to the movies this afternoon, do you?"

2. Now ask each participant to take a moment and think of something they would or would not like for themselves, or what they would or would not like to do.

3. Ask the participants to directly state their intentions to each other, avoiding words such as "might," "maybe," "could," or "possibly," Insert words such as "I want," "I'd like" or "I intend."

4. Now have the participants go beyond intentions to actions (behaviors) by having them describe their behaviors (related to their intentions) toward others–what have they done or what are they doing. Expressing intentions and actions are important because these involve a commitment to do or not to do something, and also provide a check on whether or not responsibility has been taken to follow through on commitments.

Variations: The more specifically the exercise can be tied to behavior, the more likely change will result. This exercise lends itself to role-playing, which can heighten its benefits.

Trainer's Notes: The leader may want to develop a catalog of examples of misplaced intentions, and may want to point out some of his or her blunders between intentions and missed communication or behavior.

Intentions and actions go hand and hand and should lead to greater self-awareness and improved relationships. This skill requires awareness of one's own behavior, awareness that this behavior has an impact on the behavior of others, and a communication to others about what one is doing. Disclosures are risky. The leader may want to start with safe issues to build a level of trust before proceeding into more risky areas.

52

The Hunt

Ajakai Jaya
Glen Jennings

Brief Description: This outdoor exercise is fun and builds a sense of teamwork between couples in the group or pairs in the family. Better relationships and a greater sense of spirituality are promoted by doing this exercise

Objectives:
1. To foster a sense of team effort for each couple.
2. To develop greater appreciation of nature and spirituality.
3. To create special symbolic meanings from objects in nature; these special meanings can enrich the couple in the distant future.

Materials Needed: A nature setting, good walking shoes for each person, and brightly colored armbands to designate couples.

Group Composition: Any number of couples or family members can be a team. Any group can be divided to make couples or teams for this exercise.

Time Required: Varies, but the minimum is about 45 minutes and can be up to 150 minutes.

Rationale: Many couples and families lack spirituality and a sense of ritual and specialness. This outdoor exercise can help overcome these. By engaging the couple or family with nature and team effort, they are most likely to value their relationships more.

Procedures:

1. Introduce the exercise by talking briefly about the value of spirituality and nature, and the importance of a sense of team effort in relationships.
2. Each couple or team is given matching brightly colored armbands and identical lists of things which can be found in nature. The list could include things such as "something heart shaped," "something old," "something new," "something green," "something rough," etc.
3. Couples or teams are to remain together while on the hunt. They are instructed to find a specific number of things from the list. They are to invent a special and private meaning for objects gathered while on the hunt.
4. Couples or teams are to begin at the same time and have a set time for returning to the group. The first couple or team to return to the beginning place with their objects is declared the winner.
5. Once all have returned, the group processes what they learned about themselves and each other by doing the exercise. Specifically they should discuss what it takes to make an effective team/couple.
6. In concluding this exercise, the couples are instructed to take their symbols and build a symbol in their home to remind them to value their teamwork, nature, and each other.

Variations: This exercise can be varied in many ways: where it is done (in a park, inner city, etc.); by the things placed on the list; the time allotted; how the teams are formed; etc.

Trainer's Notes: This exercise is especially meaningful if done in a remote setting and rugged terrain. The exercise is more meaningful if little emphasis is placed on the competition between couples or teams. For some groups it is wise to spend time emphasizing the importance of team effort.

SECTION FIVE: ENHANCERS

Chapter 53. **Rainbow of Feelings**

An exercise made into a game that allows adults to become more aware of young children's feelings.

Chapter 54. **Signals Bingo**

This exercise, which was adapted from bingo and roadway signs, can be used to help group or family members along the road to better and more rewarding relationships. Participants identify common roadway signals and translate the symbols and meanings to the area of the interpersonal and family relationships.

Chapter 55. **Facial Massage**

This exercise increases communication and caring within the group or family. Participants give each other a facial massage in a turn-taking manner. Touching is an innate human need, yet in many families and cultures touching is forbidden and family members are deprived of opportunities for communicating at a more meaningful level. Touching is an important part of communicating non-sexual love and caring.

Chapter 56. **Positive Affirmation**

This exercise promotes positive relationships and appreciation of self. It is appropriate for small groups or families. The participants hear and later have a record of positive comments others have said to them.

Chapter 57.   Leisure Coat of Arms

Life is enhanced whenever we become more aware of the values and beliefs we hold in the area of leisure. This exercise enhances self-identity while promoting group cohesion.

Chapter 58.   If I Could, I Would . . .

This exercise provides participants with the opportunity to explore their personal meanings of life and free time.

Chapter 59.   Treasure Box

The group or family members are asked to imagine or bring a box which contains treasures, memories, or junk saved over the years. This can be used to renew feelings and memories and can be used symbolically to work through difficult times.

Chapter 60.   Connections

By using three balls of yarn, the group or family becomes more connected; this easily results in greater appreciation of each other.

Chapter 61.   Magic Box: Increasing Leisure Activities

This is an enhancer exercise for facilitating dreams into realities and enriching life. It can increase one's repertoire of options for good times and growth.

Chapter 62.   If I Had a Hammer, I'd Hammer

Participants are helped to overcome self-doubts, myths, and obstacles. Participants receive a new lease on self-development and life by taking a solution-focused approach to problems.

Chapter 63.   Choices

By expanding ways of thinking about choices, participants put themselves on the road to a more enhanced and fun life. This exercise helps participants to become more flexible in their thinking.

53

Rainbow of Feelings

Mary Jane Clayborn
Vicki McCall
Glen Jennings
Ron McManus

Brief Description: An exercise made into a game that allows adults to become more aware of young children's feelings.

Objectives:
1. To develop more skill in reading and understanding nonverbal communication.
2. To help children become more aware of their feelings.
3. To help children learn that feelings are OK no matter what they feel.
4. To provide practice for children and parents putting words to their feelings.

Materials Needed: Two dice, a set of feelings cards for each participant, and an appropriate prize for the winner of the exercise (a small gift such as a package of balloons, fruit or a small bag of candy that can be shared with all participants).

Group Composition: Three to eight players per group; divide larger groups into subgroups.

Time Required: Thirty to 45 minutes.

Rationale: Many people and especially children often have difficulty both understanding and expressing their feelings. This exercise provides the structure for learning more about feelings and expressing those feelings. Too often adults are not aware of children's feelings, and this exercise provides opportunities for adults and especially parents to become more sensitive to the feelings of children. The exercise can be beneficial to any group whether a family, a group of children, a group of adolescents, a group of adults, a training group that is meeting for the first time, or a group that has worked together for some time. Any group who does the exercise is most likely to be closer, more understanding of each other, become better communicators, and become more productive.

Procedures:
1. Introduce the exercise with the following remarks:
    • Feelings are an important part of life.
    • It is healthy to be aware of what we are feeling at all times.
    • No matter what the feeling, it is OK.
    • There is a big difference between feeling something and acting on it.
2. Explain that this exercise is designed to help people become more aware of their feelings, to learn more about feelings, and learn to share feelings with others.
3. Next, give each player a set of feelings cards. Instruct each player to look at the set of cards and put his/her favorite feeling card at the top of the deck face up.
4. Explain that rolls of the dice indicate the following: 2 = miss a turn, 3 = tell about the feelings of a scared card, 4 = tell about the feelings of a lonely card, 5 = tell about the feelings of a sad card, 6 = tell abut the feelings of a loved card, 7 = tell about the feelings of a happy card, 8 = tell about the feelings of an angry card, 9 = tell about the feelings of a disappointment card, 10 = tell about the feelings of a hurt card, 11 = a free card and the player can choose any card to tell the feelings about, and 12 = the player gets to tell about the feelings of two cards (the two cards at the top of the players deck).
5. Each player rolls the dice, the largest number rolled is the first player to take a turn. Play proceeds clockwise around the circle of players.

6. If a player rolls the number for the top card, he/she explains why it is the favorite and the player gets a second turn. Then play moves to the next player on the left. Cards are discarded once played.
7. If a player rolls a number that does not complement the top card of his/her deck, play moves to the next player.
8. The first player to play all his/her cards is declared the winner, but play continues until all players have played all their cards.
9. Bring closure to the exercise by reviewing the objectives of the exercise with the players. As with many exercises in this handbook, it can be quite beneficial to ask participants what the exercise meant to them personally.

Variations: This exercise can be varied by making different cards and substituting them for the cards listed. Some suggestions for other cards could be: bashful, timid, overwhelmed, excited, worried, contented, anxious, irrational, bored, compassionate, hostile, pleasure, disgust, ecstasy, enthusiasm, terror, etc.

Another variation is to give each player two decks of cards, to extend the time required to play the game and allow more practice with the same feelings.

Another variation is to have players act out the feelings in a pantomime fashion. This places more importance upon understanding nonverbal communication.

Trainer's Notes: This exercise can be quite meaningful and beneficial for families and individuals who tend to intellectualize things. Some males who tend to give off macho images can find this exercise beneficial in that it helps them to get closer to others and especially their loved ones.

The trainer needs to be aware that this exercise could bring forth strong feelings around sensitive issues, e.g., the feeling of anger may have been the result of conflict between two players from a previous interchange. If this is the case, the trainer should point out to the players that this is not a problem-solving or conflict resolution exercise. In such cases, the trainer may want to later provide an opportunity for problem solving or conflict resolution.

54

Signals Bingo

Ron McManus
Glen Jennings

Brief Description: This exercise, which was adapted from bingo and roadway signs, can be used to help group or family members along the road to better and more rewarding relationships. Participants identify common roadway signals and translate the symbols and meanings to the area of the interpersonal and family relationships.

Objectives:
1. To provide an interesting and different way to think about relationships.
2. To introduce symbols that people see regularly as reminders for building better relationships.
3. To teach and reinforce concepts that are important in all caring relationships.
4. To provide an exercise that is pleasurable and helps strangers to get to know each other.

Materials Needed: An enlarged version of the Signals Bingo Card, and cards for each group or family.

Group Composition: Two to six members per group.

Time Required: Although there tends to be no specific time requirement, this exercise is usually completed in 30 to 60 minutes.

Rationale: Every day, people see traffic signals and think of them

229

only in terms of transportation and never associate them as signals for better relations with loved ones and co-workers. This exercise applies some principles from learning theory (transfer of learning) to help the participants build better relationships.

Procedures:

1. Begin the session with the following question: "Have you ever learned something new and did not have an opportunity to apply the new knowledge?"
2. Continue with the following comments:
   - People tend to remember what they see.
   - People can learn to apply what they see to their interpersonal and family situations.
3. Pass out to each person a Signals Bingo Card. Explain that this exercise is most applicable to family situations, but has application to interpersonal relations. The exercise will be used here as a discussion starter and a tool for self-reflection.
4. Divide the group into smaller groups of two to six members each.
5. Instruct everyone to read over the Signals Bingo Card silently and to put an X on any of the squares that they feel they have done or applied within the last 24 hours.
6. Group members then share with each other information about the signals crossed off their Signals Bingo Cards. After everyone has had an opportunity to talk, the group takes a new card and marks off all the squares that the members had marked on their individual cards.
7. If the group has five squares marked off in a row that are vertical, horizontal, or diagonal, the group shouts "Signals Bingo" and that group wins. As in regular Bingo, there can be more than one winner at a time.
8. If no group wins, the trainer may choose to have the groups change members and then the exercise is done again.
9. After a group has won, conclude with the following comments:
   - The exercise was a means of helping you get to know each other better.
   - The exercise should help you to think more often about interpersonal relations and to value those relations more.

- The exercise should have taught some positive concepts that you can apply to your personal life.

Variations: This exercise can be adapted easily for use by a family. The family may use the Signals Bingo Card for each member to keep a log of these activities for a specific time period, e.g., from Friday evening until Sunday evening. Each family member marks off the different squares that are done during the time period. On Sunday evening each member tells about each square that they marked off during the time period.

Another way to vary this exercise is to have the group or family members add new signals and develop appropriate meanings for each new signal added.

Trainer's Notes: This exercise could be used to get a group or family to begin the process of talking about relationships. Such a discussion could go on for a rather lengthy time and be used to develop a value hierarchy of "What We Most Value in Relationships."

If the training session is conducted in a corporate or a school setting, the group might find it beneficial to develop a set of signals to place at strategic places in their setting as a way to promote greater transfer of learning.

SIGNALS BINGO CARD

⊘ (circle with turn arrow crossed)	SLOW (diamond)	◇ oo (signal diamond)	WARNING (diamond)	⇄ (diamond with two arrows)
Always try to be close to your family members; never *turn* against those who love you.	Sometimes it is wise to remember the adage: "Be *slow* to anger."	Look for *warning signals* of a problem. Try to solve the problem before it gets worse.	Be *warned* that a harsh word said often gets a harsh word in return.	Family members can do different things and be going in *different directions* and still love each other.
TUNNEL (arch)	SHARP RIGHT (diamond with arrow)	PASS WITH CARE (rectangle)	ONE WAY ↑ (rectangle)	DETOUR AHEAD (diamond)
Tunnel vision is looking only ahead. Be alert to what is happening in your family.	*Sharp* words spoken, such as "hate" or "stupid," do more harm than they will ever do good.	Never *pass* up opportunities to express your love.	There is *one way* for families to grow closer, and that is by better communication.	Sometimes families must be willing to change their course of direction. Change can be good. A *detour* can offer new opportunities.
STOP (hexagon)	CROSSING (diamond with cross)	FREE SPACE (rectangle)	END ONE WAY (rectangle)	DO NOT PASS (rectangle)
It is often wise to *stop* and think before you speak.	A happy family does not happen by just *crossing* your fingers and hoping for the best.	Let each family member be *free* to be themselves.	Family members need to realize that they do not always agree, not always see problems in just *one way*.	*Do not pass* up opportunities to draw closer to each other.

ONE LANE

Family members need to feel that at times they are all headed together in the same direction. They need to feel as if they are *one*.

DO NOT ENTER

Do not enter into other people's business.

MERGE

A family is composed of individuals who *merge* together with concern and love.

Do not turn right away from a problem. Problems can offer opportunities.

SPEED ZONE AHEAD

Trying to live in the fast lane can be dangerous. *Speed kills.*

DANGEROUS

Drugs are *dangerous* for any family member.

SLIPPERY

Opportunities for closeness will *slip* through your fingers unless you make the most of them.

OBSTRUCTION

Sometimes our lack of listening is the biggest *obstruction* in the way of communicating with loved ones.

YIELD

Yield to the temptation of always being critical about someone else.

WINDING

Everybody needs to be alone. Take time to *wind* down from the activities and demands of the day.

Facial Massage

Glen Jennings

Brief Description: This exercise increases communication and caring within the group or family. Participants give each other a facial massage in a turn-taking manner. Touching is an innate human need, yet in many families and ethnic groups touching is forbidden and members are deprived of opportunities for communicating at a more meaningful level. Touching is an important part of communicating nonsexual love and caring.

Objectives:
1. To teach the group or family more and better ways of communicating.
2. To teach the family another way of communicating "I care about YOU and love YOU!"
3. To teach the art of massage to the trainees.
4. To debunk the idea that touching is always sexual.

Materials Needed: No materials are required. However, the exercise can be enriched and more pleasant if relaxing background music is played; a soft surface (carpet, blanket, air mattress, or bear skin rug) is available for participants to lie on; and facial lotion or baby lotion is available.

Group Composition: Any group would be appropriate.

Time Required: Forty-five to 75 minutes, depending upon the number of participants.

Rationale: For centuries the use of touch and especially therapeutic touch has been recognized as an effective adjunct to health and as a means of effective communication. Due to our cultural attitude of associating touch with sex, many families have lost the richness that can be achieved only through hugging and touching. This exercise affirms that touching is a part of family life, and that it is crucial to better communication.

Procedures:
1. The trainer needs to be aware of the need for extreme sensitivity in conducting and guiding the group through the exercise. Also be aware that some families may not be a candidate for the exercise, e.g., families with a history of abuse or sexual violations.
2. Discuss with the group the importance of contact comfort (touching, the need is innate: research suggests that infants thrive better with touch; children learn more when touched by teachers; couples who touch more report having better marriages; etc.).
3. Give special effort to debunking the idea of touch = sexual; emphasize that touching is one of the most effective means of communicating empathy, caring, love, tenderness, nurturance, comradery, friendship, etc.
4. Point out to the group that the skin is a communication medium.
5. It may be of value to some groups/families to share with them some findings from research, related to touching and the need for touching:
   • Touching of infants increases their life expectancies.
   • Infants and children are less restless after receiving contact comfort (touching).
   • Infants and children who receive touching appear to learn more rapidly than nonstimulated children.
   • Nursing home occupants report benefits from touching and rate personnel who touch as providing better care.
   • Nurses who touch are considered to provide better care and to be more friendly.

- Recovery time after serious illness and surgery is reduced with therapeutic touch.
- Contact comfort tends to reduce both physical and emotional tension.

6. The art of massage–general guidelines:
   - Begin with the use of pads of end joints of fingers and thumbs.
   - Use a moderately heavy pressure–as if pressing wrinkles out of skin.
   - Check with massagee as to whether to lighten or increase pressure.
   - Use both hands at once on parallel parts of face.

7. Facial massage procedures:
   - The massagee lies on his/her back on carpet/blanket and the massager sits on floor at head of massagee.
   - The massager starts with forehead and slowly works down from center of forehead to outside of face to chin.
   - Next, massage downward and slightly diagonally across cheek (toward nose).
   - Massage downward, around and on nose, to upper lip.
   - Massage behind ears and down to top of shoulders, then lower lip to chin, then next to front of shoulders.
   - Gently massage underside of head downward, past back of neck to base of shoulders.
   - The massager should check frequently as to the comfort of the massagee, especially in terms of pressure applied (too light? too heavy?), stroking (long or short?), sensitive areas?, etc.

8. The massager and the massagee then trade positions.

9. After all participants have had both experiences, bring closure to the exercise by leading the group in processing the experience. Finally, encourage them to try this exercise with all family members.

Variations: For variation the trainer/counselor can allow or disallow talking; by disallowing talk, emphasis is placed on touch as a form of communication. The addition of foot massage to this exercise can increase its effectiveness. The use of pleasant, relaxing music and body or facial lotion changes the mood and makes the exercise more meaningful.

Trainer's Notes: The trainer needs to be aware that some individuals and groups would be poor candidates for this exercise, e.g., abusive families, individuals from abusive families, individuals who have not become reasonably comfortable with their sexuality, and some who just never enjoy being touched. The trainer should exhibit a deeply caring and professional attitude as a part of this exercise. If the trainer is professional in manner, the participants are more likely to view this as a communication exercise.

Positive Affirmation

Glen Jennings

Brief Description: This exercise promotes positive relationships and appreciation of self. It is appropriate for small groups or families. The participants hear and later have a record of positive comments others have said to them.

Objectives:
1. To build a sense of group/family appreciation for each member.
2. To develop a greater sense of self-appreciation or self-worth.
3. To orient family/group perspectives in a positive direction.

Materials Needed: Pens, 5 × 8 unlined index cards, and file folder labels (approximately five for each participant and a few extras).

Group Composition: Ideally, the entire family should constitute the group. Positive affirmation also is appropriate for other small groups (in-service training, group activities, seminars, etc.) as a rapport or group process activity.

Time Required: Usually 45 to 75 minutes, depending upon the number of individuals in the family or group. Small families or groups of these to six members can usually complete the exercise in about 45 minutes.

Rationale: Research indicates that positive interactions are a key element in building better family relationships and individual self-esteem. This exercise is rich in positive stroking, and provides an opportunity for the family to experience positive interchanges. Some families, groups, and individuals may have had little experience in seeing each other in a positive, accepting, or supportive way. Positive affirmation is an exercise the family or group can use to change this. Positive affirmation teaches individuals how to communicate appreciation of others.

Procedures:
1. Briefly overview the importance of positive relationships and positive stroking in terms of interpersonal relationships:
   • Most people prefer to spend time with someone who is positive and appreciative of others.
   • Patients recovering from surgery heal more rapidly when cared for by positive caretakers.
   • Students learn more and maintain better emotional health when taught by appreciative teachers.
   • Research suggests that it takes at least three positives to balance one negative in behavior modification.
   • Shame is one of the most destructive things a human may experience, and appreciation is about the opposite of shame. Thus, appreciation is one of the great building blocks of human development.
2. Have the group or family sit in a rather tight circle. Divide large groups into subgroups of four to six per group.
3. Distribute a pen, an index card, and file folder labels to each participant. Give each participant as many file folder labels less one as there are members of each subgroup, i.e., each participant needs a file folder label for everyone in the group except himself/herself.
4. Instruct everyone to fold the index card in half, to make a five-by-four-inch booklet.
5. Then instruct all to write their names on the covers of the booklets. The name can be written vertically, horizontally, diagonally, or however the owner decides.
6. Instruct all to carefully think about positive characteristics of each other member of their group. They should think in terms of positive physical characteristics, social characteristics, in-

tellectual characteristics, emotional characteristics, and spiritual characteristics.

7. Give enough time for members to think of such positive characteristics for everyone in their group. It may be beneficial for them to make some brief positive notes about each other member.

8. Next, instruct each member to write the positive characteristics for each member on a file folder label. It helps if the initials of the receiver appear in the upper left corner of the label and the initials of the writer appear in the lower right corner of the label.

9. After allowing enough time for all to prepare their labels for each member of their group, the trainer says, "Now, I want you to take turns on this next part."

10. The trainer says, "I want the youngest member of each group to hand his or her booklet to the person on the left. I want that person on the left to take the booklet and stick the label they have prepared in the booklet. Then deliberately hand the booklet back to its owner and at the moment both have a hand on the booklet, stop. While both are touching the booklet, the writer of the label should look the owner of the booklet directly in the eyes and say aloud what he or she has written."

11. Caution all to avoid discrediting their positive and appreciative comments by adding qualifiers or "yes, buts—"

12. Also encourage the use of names when the writer addresses the owner of the booklet, and model some appropriate examples, such as:
   - "Sue, I like the kindness expressed in your bright brown eyes." (physical)
   - "Ted, you are one of the most thoughtful people I have known." (social)
   - "Karen, you have great problem-solving skills." (intellectual)
   - "Alex, I appreciate your calm disposition." (emotional)
   - "Linda, I always get a lift when I am around you." (spiritual)
   - "Marvin, you are a joyful person to be around." (spiritual)

- "George, you have a most understanding
    smile." (spiritual)
- "Lynn, I appreciate how you put others at ease
    so rapidly." (social)
13. Caution all to listen to each booklet exchange. Also discourage members from writing and saying the same things about each member–encourage creativity and sincerity.
14. After all have had an opportunity to share and receive from the exercise, bring closure by saying that all should feel good about themselves, feel appreciated by others, have some rich verbal memories from the exercise, and have a permanent written record that they can refer to at needed times.
15. The trainer may want to close by expressing his/her appreciation for the opportunity to share this exercise with the group.

Variations: This exercise appears to be best when there are four to six members per group, with the ideal of five members per group. Positive affirmation can be done with groups of over 30 by simply reorganizing the group into subgroups of four to six per group and spacing the groups around the area.

Trainer's Notes: The trainer should approach this exercise with a positive and caring attitude. It is important that the trainer be alert to the difficulty some individuals may have in being positive and appreciative of others.

If the trainer encounters a participant who is unable to think in positive and appreciative terms about others, this usually marks someone who would benefit from individual counseling or therapy.

This exercise is easily modified to fit specific groups, such as: teachers, ministers, etc.; and special topic groups such as grief groups, groups for the divorced, groups dealing with relationship issues, etc.

If the group members are total strangers, the trainer will need to give each group some specific topics to discuss so they can develop a sense of each other. The trainer may want to give some specific topics, such as:

- Share with the group your most meaningful experience before age five, between five and 15 years of age, 15 and 25 years of age, etc.
- Tell the group about your happiest moment, about your most frightening experience, about your proudest moment, about your saddest moment, etc.
- Describe your closest friend, your favorite song, the most touching movie or play, etc.

By talking about such topics, the participant will have a better knowledge base for the exercise.

Experience has shown that individuals have called years after being involved in this exercise to say it was one of the most meaningful experiences they have ever had.

Leisure Coat of Arms

Laura McLachlin

Brief Description: Life is enhanced whenever we become more aware of the values and beliefs we hold in the area of leisure. This exercise enhances self-identity while promoting group cohesion.

Objectives:
1. To increase awareness of personal meanings of leisure.
2. To acquaint participants with each other.
3. To discuss personal interests, values, and needs with the group or family.

Materials Needed: Copies of the Leisure Coat of Arms, and pen or pencil or coloring pencils.

Group Composition: A small group of individuals who are together for the first time or who do not know each other well. This exercise can also be implemented with families.

Time Required: Thirty to 45 minutes.

Rationale: The discovery of personal values, interests, and needs can result in strengthening self-identity and group cohesion. Communicating these attributes to others can reaffirm one's identity and teach people about each other.

Procedures:
1. Hand out a Leisure Coat of Arms form to each individual. Instruct individuals to fill out the six sections according to the following questions:

    A. What do you regard as your greatest personal achievement to date?

    B. What leisure activity do you most enjoy?

    C. What is your favorite winter sport?

    D. What would you do if you had one year to live and were guaranteed success in whatever you attempted?

    E. What leisure activity do you like to do with your family?

    F. What three things would you most like to be said of you if you died tomorrow?

2. Participants may draw or write descriptions according to their own desires. Allow three to five minutes for each question.

3. Discussion may focus on sharing of each person's coat of arms, why they chose their responses, what the entire coat of arms says about each person, the values revealed in the sixth question, etc.

Variations: Questions may be altered to fit the needs of the group or family. Participants may be asked to fill out the coat of arms as they feel their significant others might complete it. This reveals their perceptions of the others' values, interests, and needs.

To encourage creativity, markers, crayons, stickers, magazines, etc., can be supplied.

Trainer's Notes: Allow ample time for each member to share his or her coat of arms. Care should be emphasized when dealing with some of the more sensitive items. Members should be encouraged to make comments and ask questions after each individual shares his or her coat of arms.

LEISURE COAT OF ARMS

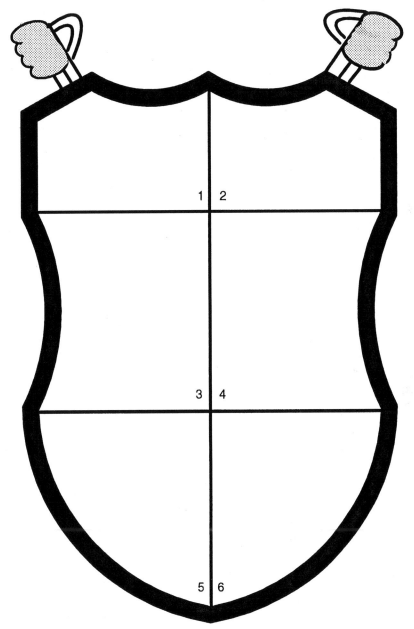

If I Could, I Would . . .

Laura McLachlin

Brief Description: This exercise provides participants with the opportunity to explore their personal meanings of life and free time.

Objectives:
1. To increase awareness of personal meanings of life and free time.
2. To facilitate discussion about individual responses.
3. To explore methods to enjoy free time and leisure time.

Materials Needed: The accompanying form and pencils or pens.

Group Composition: A small group of six to 15 people, or a family–especially an extended family.

Time Required: Thirty to 60 minutes, depending upon the number in the group and the detail of answers shared with the group.

Rationale: Developing a personal philosophy of free time and leisure is essential to the way a person spends his or her free time, and to his or her attitude toward leisure time. This exercise promotes the development of a personal leisure philosophy and contributes to examining one's philosophy of life. It has value in assisting participants to examine their priorities for life and free time.

Procedures:
1. Hand out If I Could, I Would form to each individual. Instruct each person to complete the sentences as they apply to him/her.

Participants should be asked to work quickly and not ponder a long time on answers. Allow approximately 15 minutes for completion.

2. After completion of the form, the discussion may center around participant responses, how the actual answers differ from how the person would want to ideally respond, how to get the most out of free time, how to do more of what they want to do, etc.

Variations: Sentences may be changed to meet the needs of a particular group, family, or session theme.

Trainer's Notes: The trainer should encourage participants to explore their personal philosophies of free time and of life. How personal philosophies differ or are similar to other group or family members' philosophies could be discussed.

IF I COULD, I WOULD . . .

Complete each sentence as it applies to you. Work as quickly as possible.

1. If this next weekend were a three-day weekend, I would want to

_____

2. I feel most proud when_____

3. My bluest days are_____

4. My favorite vacation dream is_____

5. One of my most joyful days was_____

6. The next rainy day I would like to_____

7. I feel best when_____

8. I would like to live in_____

9. If I used my free time more wisely, I would_____

10. I really feel proud when I_____

11. On vacations, I like to_____

12. I feel bored when_____

13. If I could visit two museums I would_____

14. If I could interview two people from history they would be____

_____

15. I am best at_____

16. If I could be in a television show, I would play_____

17. If I could be a professional athlete, it would be in_____

18. If I could have a subscription to two magazines, I would choose

_____

19. One of my greatest accomplishments was_____

20. I get great pleasure from_____

21. What I want most in life is to_____

22. One of my greatest strengths is_____

23. Someday I would like to_____

24. If I could be any age, I would be_____

25. One of my most exciting experiences was_____

26. I am attracted to people who_____

27. I would like to see my family change_____

28. To me it would be extremely dangerous to_____

29. I feel most loved when_____

30. Often I find myself wondering if_____

31. It would be fun to take a train to_____

32. I would like to vacation in_____

33. The trouble with being polite is_____

34. I would like for my family to get together to_____

35. The most frightening thing about getting close to another is____

_____

36. A group I would enjoy being a member of is_____

37. What the world needs now is_____

38. Healthy families_____

59

Treasure Box

Stephen Freeman

Brief Description: The group or family members are asked to imagine or bring a box which contains treasures, memories, or junk saved over the years. This can be used to renew feelings and memories and be used symbolically to work through difficult times.

Objectives:
1. To help express emotions and gain a sense of concreteness.
2. To help promote change and integrate strengths.
3. To provide a vehicle for expressing memories and feelings.

Materials Needed: Members are instructed to bring a box of junk or treasures.

Group Composition: Small group or family.

Time Required: Thirty to 60 minutes, depending upon the number in the group or family.

Rationale: Treasure or junk boxes include symbolism, sensory modes, visions, and nonverbal expressions. These contribute to the expression of feelings long forgotten that can resurface and help bring about healing, renewal, and change.

Procedures:
1. Make the following comments to the group: Treasure boxes or junk boxes exist in all of our lives. They give meaning to life. Memories and boxes can be mixed, happy, sad, pain-filled,

exciting, etc. Memories and boxes affect present relationships. They need to be rediscovered and used to enrich our development.

2. Point out that each member is free not to speak until safety is felt.

3. Group members take turns taking an object from their treasure boxes. They should look at the object as they have never looked at it before, and then describe it in the minutest detail.

4. The sharing progresses until every group member who desires has had a chance to tell about a treasure. The sharing may go around the group more than once.

5. Lead a brief discussion centered around the feelings that evolved as members shared, and around what members learned about each other.

6. The trainer or a member may bring closure to the exercise by making a few summary remarks.

Variations: The group or family may choose to draw pictures of their treasures, or may bring in boxes with feeling words placed in them. The members would then proceed to describe the objects that evoke these feelings.

Trainer's Notes: The trainer may need to help the group members realize they are talking about themselves as they describe the object. Also, many feelings may come up which may have to be dealt with before dismissing the group or family.

60

Connections

Ajakai Jaya
Glen Jennings

Brief Description: By using three balls of yarn, the group or family becomes more connected; this easily results in greater appreciation of each other.

Objectives:
1. To foster a sense of positiveness and self-esteem.
2. To promote a sense of togetherness.

Materials Needed: Three balls of different colored string or yarn.

Group Composition: Any number of people from three to eight is adequate for this exercise. Larger groups can be divided into subgroups of three to eight.

Time Required: Fifteen to 60 minutes, depending upon the trainer's discretion and ability to move the group through the exercise.

Rationale: Having a sense of being valued and appreciated is crucial to all wholesome relationships. When humans are valued by others, they have better self-concepts, and are more beautiful and more competent. This exercise creates a sense of being valued.

Procedures:
1. Group members sit in a close circle facing each other. Then the trainer briefly talks about the importance of positive communication, valuing others, and connections.

2. The first person begins by wrapping a piece of yarn around his/her finger and offers a compliment to another group member, who then takes the yarn and wraps it around his/her finger as well.
3. The second person then speaks to a third, and so on. The yarn becomes a network, and a first round is completed when all members have heard something complimentary about themselves, and have spoken to others.
4. A second round begins with another color of yarn and this thought to be completed by each member: "You were helpful to me when_____ ." The second round continues the way the first round was played.
5. A third round begins with the final color of yarn and this thought to be completed by each member: "My hope for you is_____ ." The third round continues the way the first and second rounds were played.
6. The final phase of this exercise is to reflect upon the obvious network in front of the group. The group ends with the removal of the yarn.

Variations: This exercise can be varied by the number of rounds played, the sentence stems used in the different rounds, and what use is made of the compliments,, e.g., they could be put on paper and saved for future reference. Other complimentary stems could be: "My hope for being in this group_____ ." "What I need from this group is _____ ." "What I most value about you is _____ ." "I appreciate you _____ ." "Your sense of caring is evident _____ ." Etc.

Trainer's Notes: Begin the exercise by talking about positive communication, valuing others, the importance of a sense of appreciation, and how all humans are in things together. If anyone contributes negative remarks, caution him or her that this is to be a positive focus.

61

Magic Box: Increasing Leisure Activities

Laura McLachlin

Brief Description: This is an enhancer exercise for facilitating dreams into realities and enriching life. It can increase one's repertoire of options for good times and growth.

Objectives:
1. To increase participants' leisure awareness.
2. To increase participants' leisure planning and decision-making skills.
3. To assist participants in identifying leisure barriers.

Materials Needed: Small box, preferably covered with black, sparkly, or mystical paper.

Group Composition: Small group or family.

Time Required: Thirty to 60 minutes.

Rationale: To expand a person's repertoire of leisure activities, risks need to be taken to implement changes. These risks begin with dreaming about experiences in which a person has always wanted to participate, but has not had the appropriate resources. This exercise encourages individuals to identify desired activities and assists in exploring the necessary requirements for participating in those desired activities.

Procedures:
1. Participants are seated or standing in a circle. The trainer hides the Magic Box and tells the group, "When you hold the Magic

Box, it contains all of those leisure activities that you have always wanted to do but never have."

2. The leader then passes the Magic Box to the person to his/her left and asks that person to open the Magic Box and tell the group what activities are inside.

3. Discussion may include why there are so many (or so few) leisure activities in the Magic Box, and planning how to get more of the activities out of the Magic Box.

4. Play continues until each participant has had a turn at opening the Magic Box.

Variations: Participants may be asked to tell what hidden talents they have that are not being utilized.

This can be an effective tool for group problem solving. Encourage group members to work together to resolve problems with leisure barriers and resources.

Trainer's Notes: The trainer may "open" the Magic Box first to make the activity less threatening. A nonjudgmental attitude by trainer and participants will help participants answer honestly.

For some groups who have little experience with revealing dreams or fantasizing, the trainer may need to talk about the healthy aspects of being free to dream and fantasize, i.e., license the members to dream or make believe.

If I Had a Hammer, I'd Hammer

Stephen Freeman

Brief Description: Participants are helped to overcome self-doubts, myths, and obstacles. Participants receive a new lease on self-development and life by taking a solution-focused approach to problems.

Objectives:
1. To generate a consciousness that we are not usually immobilized or stymied by things but more often by our thoughts about things.
2. To help participants identify goals and identify the attitudes ("If I only had_____ , I could_____ ") that prevent them from attaining their goals.
3. To acknowledge the universality of fear, self-doubt, lack of confidence, etc., but also to acknowledge that it is only when we act as if this were true that we do immobilize ourselves.

Materials Needed: A designated recorder with pen and paper to take notes of participants' responses.

Group Composition: This exercise can be used with individuals, couples, families, or a group.

Time Required: For a couple, family, or small group, the time required is 15 to 25 minutes. As the size of the group increases there is an increase in time of approximately four to six minutes per person.

Rationale: By asking individuals (families or groups) to complete an "if_____ then _____ " statement, they begin to overcome their largest obstacles–themselves. Having them identify what they would do differently "if_____ then_____ " helps to prescribe the behavior necessary for attainment, or approximate attainment, of the desired outcomes. An analogy would be: One need only look at a Bumble Bee to see–you gotta believe–poor Bumble Bee doesn't know if only it weren't so unaerodynamic, it could fly.

Procedures:
1. The leader selects someone to be the recorder. The recorder writes down the participants' responses.
2. Ask each individual to identify something he/she has been unable to accomplish but desires to do.
3. Then ask what attributes would be necessary for him/her to accomplish the desired thing.
4. Ask each participant what he/she would do differently if it were true that he/she possessed the necessary attributes.
5. Give each participant a list from the recorder of the things he/she aspires to, but has been unable to accomplish. Also give each the list of needed attributes and his/her responses as to how he/she (possessing the attributes) would behave differently.
6. Ask each individual to commit for the next week (variable time) to act as if he/she had these attributes, and then return to the group with a report on what happened.

Variations: One variation of this exercise is to audio record the exercise and have members analyze their blocks and how they set themselves up for failure. By role-playing some of the behaviors, there is more likely to be a transfer to everyday life.

Trainer's Notes: The more members talk about how things would be different, the more likely things will be different. Some people have great difficulty thinking in terms of how things could be different. Give them plenty of time and encouragement.

Some groups benefit by looking at the connections between thinking, behaving, and feeling. Point out that as we change one aspect of our thinking, behaving, and feeling cycle, the others parts of the cycle will change.

Keep aspirations within the realm of reason and beware of sabotage and "But if" behaviors. Don't tolerate "I can't." Remember, we're only acting.

Choices

Lee Hipple

Brief Description: By expanding ways of thinking about choices, participants put themselves on the road to a more enhanced and fun life. This exercise helps participants to become more flexible in their thinking.

Objectives:
1. To develop skills in thinking about choices.
2. To clarify for each individual life situations where he or she can make choices, and life situations where choices are made for him or her.
3. To develop feelings of self-control and personal power.
4. To teach the process of brainstorming.

Materials Needed: None, unless the trainer wants to write choices down on a flip chart.

Group Composition: The ideal number of participants can vary from three to eight. Larger groups can be accommodated by limiting the time for individual responses and the number of examples developed.

Time Required: Time will vary depending on how the exercise is structured and the amount of depth pursued with each person. At a minimum, each person should have two to three minutes for the first part of the exercise and five minutes for the second part. If done in a group setting, this exercise can easily take 20 to 45 minutes.

Rationale: Children, adolescents, and adults often see themselves as powerless and as being completely bound by the authority of others such as parents, teachers, police, supervisors, etc. Children and adolescents also often see themselves as having very limited choices, or perhaps as having no choices at all. Also, many children and adolescents have not been taught how to make choices, or how to use the process of "brainstorming" to increase their awareness of the choices available to them.

Procedures:

1. Introduce the exercise with the following remarks:
   - Choices are an important part of life.
   - Each of us has had life situations where a choice was made for us by someone else.
   - Each of us has life situations where we can make our own choices.
   - Many times we don't know the difference between these two situations, and we waste a lot of energy trying to change situations that we can't change or by being angry about those situations that we can't change.
   - Many times we don't feel in control of our own lives and we don't know how to make choices.
2. Then explain: This exercise is designed to help you become aware of the things you can make choices about and the things you can't make choices about, and, in the process of doing the exercise, you may find that you have more choices in your life than you thought you had.
3. Start by giving the group an example of something that you could not make a choice about; for example: the people who are your parents; how many brothers and sisters you have; whether you are male or female; how tall you are.
4. Next, give the group an example of something you can make a choice about; for example: what kind of work you do; where you live; what clothes you wear.
5. Then ask each person in the group to articulate something he/she has a choice about, and something he/she does not have a choice about.
6. After everyone has had a turn, give the group an example of a situation you found yourself in where you had to make a choice about how you would act. Briefly describe the situation

and the various alternative choices, ending with the question: "Or–???" For example:

Yesterday I was driving my car on the way to work and some guy pulled out in front of me. I had to slam on my brakes and I was really mad. I had several choices; I could have honked my horn at him, I could have made an obscene gesture at him, I could have thought to myself he was a crummy driver, or–???

Then encourage the group to brainstorm about other choices that you had.

7. Group members then take turns to explain situations they were in recently where they had choices and tell what they saw their choices to be, ending with "Or–???" Other group members then brainstorm about additional choices they see as having been available for each person. The trainer might even decide to help get the first person started by giving a few examples of problem situations people have, for example: someone calls you stupid, you are chosen last to be on a team, someone you care about is drunk and begins to scream at you, etc.

8. In each situation, guide the group in differentiating between those things that people really can't decide for themselves and those things where they can make choices. For example, all of us can decide how we will act in any situation. If someone makes us mad we might want to hit them but we don't have to; we can make another choice. We can stop, think, and make a choice. That choice might be to wait and hit them later or tell them off later. Or we might do something entirely different. The point is we don't have to act/react spontaneously and fly off the handle. We can think of other ways to act, even if we are upset, or excited, or scared, or hurt.

Variations: This exercise can be changed by asking each group member to talk about what happens after he/she makes a choice. Again the trainer might give an example of a situation, a choice, and a result and then ask each group member to do the same. This might be prefaced by talking about the fact that before we choose to act one way or the other, we need to think of what will happen later. For example, if you choose not to do your homework, you might get in trouble. Before you choose not to do it, you should think ahead to this trouble.

Trainer's Notes: This exercise can be helpful for children, adolescents, or adults who tend to think of themselves as having few choices. It can also be a frustrating exercise for those persons who tend to utilize only a very limited repertoire of behaviors and who do not want those behaviors challenged.

SECTION SIX:
ENERGIZERS

Chapter 64. **Ways I Want to Grow**

This exercise focuses on ways in which the individual wants to grow. It can be directed to growth within the group, family, or simply for personal reasons. Participants publicly state one area in which they wish to improve, then another member imagines aloud to the group how things would be different as a result of the growth.

Chapter 65. **Look Alike**

This energizer is an exercise for the group or family when they have become tired or bored with other activities. The exercise requires half the members to identify another member who looks like some family member. After identifying the "look alike," the identifier gives the look alike a soothing back rub.

Chapter 66. **The Timer Method**

This structured exercise improves listening and expressiveness in emotionally charged situations. It helps individuals recognize the self-defeating nature of the typical fighting style, which emphasizes personal gain (winning) rather than resolving the conflict.

Chapter 67. **Values for All Humankind**

This exercise has participants publicly state a value they hold dear and believe if practiced by all of humankind, it would create a better world.

Chapter 68.   Four Corners

A return trip to the feelings of adolescence helps in understanding others as well as self. Participants choose one of four feelings which was common during adolescence to share with others.

Chapter 69.   Expanding Skills: Personal Growth

In this exercise, the group or family members help each other to identify personal skills. Then the group assists each participant to think in terms of transferring the skills to other areas of his or her life.

Chapter 70.   Repertoire of Songs

Awareness of others' feelings, values, preferences, and moods can facilitate communication and understanding. The more diverse the participants, the more likely tolerance will be an outcome of this exercise.

Chapter 71.   What Kind of Person Are You?

This exercise helps bring congruence to perceptions of self by self and by others. By achieving greater congruence between the way we see ourselves and the way others see us, the more likely we are to improve our relationships.

Ways I Want to Grow

Glen Jennings

Brief Description: This exercise focuses on ways in which the individual wants to grow. It can be directed to growth within the group, family, or simply for personal reasons. Participants publicly state one area in which they wish to improve, then another member imagines aloud to the group how things would be different as a result of the growth.

Objectives:
1. To have individuals make a public statement of ways in which they would like to grow.
2. To build group/family solidarity through self-revelation.
3. To provide a basis for understanding each other better.

Materials Needed: A flip chart or chalkboard for recording each participant's statement of growth.

Group Composition: The ideal number of participants can vary from four to 15. If there are more than 15, the group should be divided into smaller subgroups. The participants can be individuals, groups, families, or a department of an agency or company.

Time Required: The time required with small groups is brief (ten to 20 minutes), but with larger groups more time is required (30 to 45 minutes).

Rationale: There is research that suggests that goals made in a public setting are more likely to be achieved than goals not publicly stated. By making a public statement, the individual becomes motivated to follow through with some behavioral changes which support the public statement. The public statement also helps secure the group's support for change.

Procedures:
1. Give a brief overview about the benefits for setting goals for personal growth:
   • Goals direct energy.
   • Goals direct personal development.
   • People with goals tend to be more successful than people lacking goals.
   • Aspirations are a key component of building self-esteem.
2. Ask the participants to think of ways in which they might want to grow to help themselves or the group. Allow a few moments for the participants to think.
3. Encourage all to give serious thoughts to one specific way in which they would like to grow or change.
4. Give some examples of statements about growth that can serve as a model for the participants, such as:
   • "I want to be more task-oriented at my work station and reserve visiting for break periods."
   • "I want to grow more pleasant in dealing with people."
   • "I want to grow closer to my children."
   • "I want to grow by being a better listener."
   • "I want to grow by putting things in their proper place, instead of piling things up."
   For some groups or families it can be helpful to suggest that they use the following sentence stem or one similar: "I want to grow by_____ ."
5. Ask each participant to share with the group an "I want to grow_____ ." statement. The trainer or a volunteer should record the statement on a flip chart or chalkboard.
6. After all participants have had an opportunity to state the way they would like to grow and the statements have been recorded, ask for a volunteer to share with the group his/her vision of the person after the growth. Emphasize the impor-

tance of being positive in stating the vision of how the person would be after the growth occurs.

7. Bring closure to this exercise by sharing with the group an anecdote about your own growth and development. The anecdote should be comparable to some of the examples the group has shared.
8. Finally, thank the group for sharing their dreams of growth, and commend them for the courage to publicly state this important part of themselves with others.

Variations: A meaningful variation of this exercise is to ask participants to make brief notes or name tags with their growth statements on them. Then they should wear their name tags for the remainder of the training session, or on specific days of the week for a set time period, e.g., wear their tags on Wednesday of each week for the next six weeks.

Another variation of this exercise is to have each person identify the major challenges he or she would have to overcome to successfully make the changes he or she has identified.

Exercises such as this can be extended by having participants keep diaries or logs of their growth achievements. If the group is an ongoing group, they could periodically review their growth plans or bring their logs to share with the group.

Trainer's Notes: The trainer should set a positive tone for the exercise and caution participants about the importance of keeping things on a positive level. This is not the time to challenge others, to try to resolve problems, or to work on personality differences. See other sections of this handbook for problem-solving and conflict resolution exercises.

There are many possibilities for modifying this exercise for use with different groups and in different settings. It has often been useful as a change of pace exercise for lengthy workshops, especially consulting workshops, which focus on improving productivity or departmental issues.

–65–

Look Alike

Robin Jennings

Brief Description: This energizer is an exercise for the group or family when they have become tired or bored with other activities. The exercise requires half the members to identify another member who looks like some family member. After identifying the "look alike," the identifier gives the look alike a soothing back rub.

Objectives:
1. To energize the group/family after some intense work.
2. To provide release for fatigue and create freshness.
3. To provide an opportunity to make a personal contact with another group/family member.

Materials Needed: None.

Group Composition: A group/family of 12 or more members; smaller groups limit the options of finding a "look alike" member. The exercise is less meaningful with small families but can be quite successful with family reunions or large groups.

Time Required: Allow ten to 20 minutes for the exercise; the time requirement does not vary with the group number. It is an appropriate exercise for breaks in workshops or seminars, or after activities requiring concentration and sitting.

Rationale: The exercise requires interaction between group members. It provides a vehicle for making a strong personal connection as the members talk about family look alikes and touch each other by giving the upper back massage. Participants tend to remember this experience and the other person permanently.

Procedures:
1. Ask all participants on one side (right) of the room to identify someone on the other side (left) of the room who looks like a family member not present at the time.
2. Allow time for all to look the other participants over for a "look alike." Suggest that they may want to identify more than one person as someone else may have selected their "look alike."
3. Select someone from the audience on whom to demonstrate the back rub. While demonstrating, explain the following:
   • Some like a back rub with a light touch and others like a heavy touch; ask your massagee what kind he or she likes.
   • Some like strokes across the back muscles while others like strokes with the back muscles. Check for preferences.
   • The important thing in giving a soothing back rub is to listen to the massagee's preference.
4. Direct the members on the right side of the room to go across to the left side and introduce themselves to their selected "look alike," tell the other persons who they look like, and then to give the "look alikes" gentle back massages.
5. After allowing a brief time for the exercise, close the exercise by pointing out that this appears to have refreshed the group. This is usually followed by a break for refreshment and rest room use.

Variations: This exercise is especially effective with groups coming together for the first time. It has been used with companies in which people from across a region or district who have talked by phone come together for the first time. Such people know each other but do not know each other (the impersonal nature of phone conversations).

For variety during the next break, the trainer can give the group on the opposite side of the room an opportunity to identify a "look alike" from the other side.

Trainer's Notes: The trainer should be prepared for someone who may say that there is no one present who looks like a family member. These people can be instructed to simply pair up and talk a few moments, then to give the back rub. Also be prepared for a group with an odd number. In this case the trainer can be a member for the exercise.

The Timer Method

Peggy Avent
Ron McManus

Brief Description: This structured exercise improves listening and expressiveness in emotionally charged situations. It helps individuals recognize the self-defeating nature of the typical fighting style, which emphasizes personal gain (winning) rather than listening and conflict resolution.

Objectives:
1. To teach a method for resolving conflict.
2. To improve both listening and expressiveness skills.

Materials Needed: A small three-minute timer (hourglass type).

Group Composition: Small groups or families.

Time Required: Fifteen to 30 minutes.

Rationale: Most people approach conflict resolution with limited skills and a mindset of "either I win or I lose." This approach limits the outcome of conflict situations. This exercise helps individuals feel assured that they will be able to express their feelings and wishes as well as achieve a mutually desirable solution without a disruptive argument. The timer method helps individuals move to "we both can win."

Procedures:
1. Share with the participants the limitations of some methods of conflict resolution, such as:

- Most people see conflict resolution as a "me versus them" situation.
- To see conflict resolution as a "win or lose" situation limits the outcome.
- Many people have difficulty listening because they are busy thinking of what they are going to say to the other person (this is called monologing).
- Often some individuals enter conflict resolution with a very limited view of the solutions acceptable.

2. Ask, "Would you like to learn a different method of conflict resolution?"

3. Introduce the exercise by saying, "This method of conflict and resolution has three parts to it. The three are: *Preparation, Confrontation,* and *The Timer Method.* Now, I will outline the three parts."

4. *Preparation:*

    a. Write down the problem so that you can organize your thoughts and clearly state what is on your mind. Note specific examples.

    b. Write out the reasons for your feelings. Don't cloud the issue with unimportant issues. Consider how your own actions may affect the problem. Be open to the possibility that you may be contributing to the problem.

    c. Brainstorm a variety of solutions to the problem. Be prepared to add to the list.

    d. Put your complaint in the form of an "*I message.*" This is not an accusing statement but an honest expression of your underlying need, want, or feeling. Ask yourself, *"What do I really want to happen?", "What do I really need?",* or *"What do I really feel?"*

    e. Look for an appropriate time and place where you can be alone without distractions. Confrontations should be private to reduce embarrassment or side-taking.

    f. If there is not a good time when you can be alone, use the steps below to arrange one.

5. *Confrontation:*

    a. Face the person. If possible and appropriate, touch him/her to get his/her attention and reinforce your words.

b. Look the person in the eye.

c. Keep a concerned, serious expression on your face.

d. Your posture and gestures should also express concern and seriousness.

e. Ask the person, *"Can I talk with you for a minute?"*

f. If the person refuses, express how important the talk is to you and ask for a specific time when you can talk: *"It's very important to me. Can we talk in an hour?"*

6. *The Timer Method:*

a. Take turns expressing facts and feelings. The person presenting the conflict issue will begin and will have three minutes to express what he/she doesn't like, reasons for concern, what he/she does like. During this three-minute period, "I statements" are to be use.

b. The other person is to listen with the intent of being able to repeat back to the first person what was said. The second person's job is to listen attentively; if necessary the second person may take notes so he/she can identify what the first person has said.

c. After three minutes, the first person will ask the second person to repeat verbatim as much of his/her statement as possible.

d. If the second person can repeat the first person's statement, he/she most likely can identify with the conflict issues. If so, then he/she should try to summarize the first person's feelings about the issues.

e. If the second person cannot repeat the first person's statement of issues, the first person should have another three minutes to repeat his/her concerns. Again the second person is given an opportunity to repeat the first person's concerns and show some understanding of his/her feelings.

f. Even if the speaker (originator of the confrontation) is not satisfied after this second explanation, the two will reverse roles. The second person will have three minutes to state the view of the conflict issues and his/her feelings. Again, "I messages" should be used in stating all grievances.

   g. The preceding steps are followed as the second person has two opportunities to state his/her concerns and check the listening skills of the first person.

   h. After each person has had two opportunities to state their concerns, and if the other person has not been able to repeat his/her issues, both are given one more opportunity to state their concerns. If after all this there remains a deadlock, the two people should move to the next (following) step.

   i. Brainstorm solutions to the problem. During the brainstorming part, remember that all ideas are listed and not evaluated at the moment they are suggested. It is important to think of unusual and extreme solutions during the brainstorming part. *No solution is stupid during the brainstorming part of problem solving.*

   j. Write all solutions down during the brainstorming part. Later the solutions can be evaluated and the most acceptable one tried.

   k. Make a resolution about the problem. If no solution was arrived at, make a resolution to continue to meet and try to resolve issues. If a solution was arrived at, make a resolution to meet again and discuss how it is working out.

   l. Thank the person for listening. If possible, shake hands or touch in some way to seal the agreement.

7. The trainer brings closure to the exercise by pointing out the advantages of the new method:

- It provides a way to resolve conflict in which both parties win.
- This method promotes better relationships by reducing problems and resentments.
- The skills learned can be used in other relationships, thus improving all communication.
- Any time we improve listening skills we become more effective with others.

Variations: One variation of this exercise is to have the two parties hold hands and look each other in the eye as each takes a turn stating his/her issues.

Trainer's Notes: During the early part of this training exercise it is important to emphasize that each speaker has three minutes of uninterrupted time to state his/her issues. During the initial training session the trainer may have to instruct the listener to listen and not interrupt; interrupting is one of the habits that is a part of ineffective conflict resolution for many people.

For large group training, the trainer should make some provisions for all participants to practice this new way of resolving conflict. It could be helpful for participants to come back to the large group and process their experiences (i.e., tell what *The Timer Method* means in terms of their personal experiences).

The trainer should be aware that at times participants may bring to training sessions issues which are emotionally loaded to the point that they require outside individual professional help. In such situations, the trainer should be prepared to make a referral or schedule these persons for individual help.

67

Values for All Humankind

Glen Jennings

Brief Description: This exersise has participants publicly state a value they hold dear and believe if practiced by all of humankind, it would create a better world.

Objectives:
1. To have each individual identify a value they hold dear.
2. To have participants publicly state the value they hold dear.
3. By publicly stating their values, participants become energized.
4. To help participants connect with others at a core level.

Materials Needed: None, unless the trainer wants to record the list of values on a flip chart.

Group Composition: Any number of participants between three and 25 is appropriate, depending upon the time available. Larger groups could be involved if divided into subgroups. This exercise can be used with all ages, and is appropriate for mixed age groups from children to senior citizens.

Time Required: Fifteen minutes is appropriate for a small group/family, but as the number of participants increase beyond six to eight members, the time increases about one minute per person.

Rationale: Values reflect our inner most personality characteristics and connect us with our ideals. Our deepest universal values are often so personal that they are not shared with others, yet they reflect the most beautiful aspects of our personhood. Most people find a great deal in common when we publicly state our values; we connect with others in more meaningful ways. This exercise helps members of the group/family to see the good in others.

Procedures:
1. Ask all to think of one of the values they hold most dear; the value should not be a religious, but rather a universal value that would cross religious lines.
2. Instruct participants to think in terms of why they cherish these values and what it would mean if all of humankind were to practice these values.
3. Then ask for volunteers who will share their values and why they cherish it with the group/family.
4. Ask the group/family to entertain some of the following questions:
   - What would this group/family be like if we lived by these values every day?
   - How would we be different if we lived by these values?
   - What would be the challenges of living by these values?
   - What would it require for this group/family to select a few of these values to implement in daily living?
   - Should this group/family live by these values?
   - Can this group/family live by these values?
   - What does this sharing of values mean to you personally?
5. Bring closure by reflecting on the quality of the group as exemplified by the values stated. Also challenge the group/family to implement the values.

Variations: The stated values could be written on a flip chart so all could see the values of the group/family. Later a copy of the values could be distributed so all would have a permanent list of them.

Trainer's Notes: The use of a flip chart can enhance the impact of this exercise. The trainer should be aware of the sensitivity whenever individuals share something this personal. Occasionally some individuals may exhibit some remorse or guilt for not living up to the values they identify and publicly state. It is usually best not to dwell on this remorse but to keep the group/family active with the current exercise.

68

Four Corners

Linda J. Brock

Brief Description: A return trip to the feelings of adolescence helps in understanding others as well as self. Participants choose one of four feelings which was common during adolescence to share with others.

Objectives:
1. To develop a sense of shared experience.
2. To develop an appreciation of people's differences.

Materials Needed: None.

Group Composition: A group of at least ten adults. This exercise works well with very large groups.

Time Required: Ten to 15 minutes.

Rationale: People feel closer when they share something personal. Many believe the way they experienced a situation is the norm, and they benefit from reminders of the individuality of each person.

Procedures:
1. Explain that the participants will be forming four groups by moving to the four corners of the room.
2. Ask the participants to think back to their teen years and remember how they felt and how adults related to them.
3. Ask them to select a corner of the room based on which phrase best describes their own adolescence.

4. Indicate the four choices, pointing out the four corners of the room:
   - Behavior problems.
   - Smooth sailing.
   - Calm outside, stormy inside.
   - Shy.
5. After participants have moved to their chosen corners, suggest they think about the following:
   - How hard was it to choose a corner?
   - How surprised were you at other participants' choices?
   - How much have you changed since adolescence?
   - How much difference is there between how teens see themselves and how adults see them?
6. Bring closure to the exercise by making a few summary statements of what the group has said about the experience.

Variations: Although this exercise can be used to help any group get acquainted, it is especially useful as an introduction to the topic of adolescence. Parents, teachers, counselors, youth group volunteers, health care professionals, and others who live or work with teens will find this exercise useful. The exercise could also be adapted for use with a group of teens, or a group of teens and their parents.

Trainer's Notes: This exercise can easily be modified for use with groups or families by changing the focus from adolescence to any of a number of different focuses, such as:

- feelings associated with the first day on a new job–eager, tentative, assured, scared;
- feelings at the time of the loss of a loved one–angry, overwhelmed, relieved, dazed;
- feelings associated with a notice of transfer–joyful, disappointed, saddened, lost;
- feelings at the time of divorce–angry, hurt, free, abandoned;
- feelings at the time of the birth of a child–relieved, ecstatic, depressed, overwhelmed.

Depending upon the nature of the group and the overall objectives for the training sessions, this exercise can be quite timely in helping the participants to break the ice (get to know each other better).

This exercise can be very powerful when used to address controversial issues with multiple families. The families will usually see that there is no consensus within and across families on such issues as curfew time, roles, dating behavior, school, etc. The exercise can be especially helpful in helping rigid families to moderate their positions on issues and to resolve power struggles.

The exercise can be modified by having the room thought of as a continuum, with opposite sides being opposite ends of the continuum. With this modification, participants can take a one-fourth position, a half position, a three-fourths position, or any position along the continuum. This type of modification is especially appropriate when the focus is on value-laden issues. The participants can be encouraged to state their positions on the values, thus helping others to see different aspects around the value concept.

Expanding Skills: Personal Growth

Laura McLachlin

Brief Description: In this exercise, the group or family members help each other to identify personal skills. Then the group assists each participant to think in terms of transferring the skills to other areas of his or her life.

Objectives:
1. To assist participants to translate their present skills to other areas of their lives.
2. To increase group interaction and cohesiveness.
3. To increase planning and decision-making skills.

Materials Needed: Paper and pencils, chalkboard or newsprint for recording group suggestions.

Group Composition: Small group (four to12 members) or family.

Time Required: Thirty to 90 minutes.

Rationale: Sometimes people are not aware of how their skills translate to activities or other areas of their lives. Group/family members can assist in the process of identifying possible skills which can be translated to other areas of one's life. This exercise creates feelings of support and positive concern for group/family members.

Procedures:
1. Instruct participants to write down three skills or attributes they feel they possess. In turn, each individual tells the group what he/she has written down. For each individual, the group brainstorms with the individual several activities or areas of life that would use those skills. The trainer should write activities as they are mentioned and have the individual write them down.
2. The trainer may want to have each individual sign a "contract" to try/participate in a certain number of activities within a specified time period.
3. Discussion may center around additional things it would take (partners, equipment, etc.) to participate in the brainstormed activities or areas. Focus on planning and decision-making skills.

Variations: Successive sessions could include discussions about how individuals have incorporated new skills into their lives.

If spending more time together as a group or family is a goal, this aspect could be included in a "contract."

Trainer's Notes: Create an atmosphere of helpfulness and positive concern for the individual. Ensure that each participant has a list of the ideas generated during the session.

Repertoire of Songs

Stephen Freeman

Brief Description: Awareness of others feelings, values, preferences, and moods can facilitate communication and understanding. The more diverse the participants, the more likely tolerance will be an outcome of this exercise.

Objectives:
1. To examine and discuss differences.
2. To share one's preferences and be able to explain them to others.
3. To help improve relationships, cohesion, and self-discovery.
4. To foster value tolerance and respect for others.

Materials Needed: A tape player, compact disc player, or record player and copies of favorite music.

Group Composition: Small group or family.

Time Required: Thirty to 75 minutes depending upon the number of participants.

Rationale: Music has been described as a therapeutic agent by which people express themselves, and it can help people to establish relationships, express moods, relax, or become invigorated. Music contributes to the expression of emotions. Music has often been described as the universal language that can be used to bring all of humankind together.

Procedures:

1. The trainer opens the exercise with the following comments:
   a. Learning how to communicate and express one's feelings is sometimes difficult even within the familiarity of one's family or group.
   b. Music sometimes expresses our feelings for us.
   c. The following exercise provides a music format to help individuals share feelings in a safe way.
2. Each player has chosen beforehand two to four minutes of their favorite music.
3. The trainer asks for a volunteer to go first.
4. The volunteer plays the song while other participants listen. Then the player proceeds to share what feelings the music evoked, why the music was chosen, and whether there is any difference between the feelings today and other times the music was played.
5. The other participants then have a chance to share any memories, feelings, or images they experienced while the music played.
6. The next volunteer plays a song and responds to it.
7. Play continues until all participants have had an opportunity to share.
8. The trainer brings closure to the exercise by making a short summary statement about the sharing and what has occurred in the group.

Variations: This exercise can be adapted easily for use by any group. The participants may choose to bring the lyrics to their songs and share them with the group. Or groups members may choose to write a few lines about the meaning of the song they heard. Rather than using music, participants may choose their favorite book, poem, saying, picture, etc.

Trainer's Notes: The trainer needs to anticipate some adjustments that may be required due to the vast differences in groups (age, educational level, ethnicity, etc.). Adjustments may be necessary due to differences in communication skills of group members.

What Kind of Person Are You?

Laura McLachlin

Brief Description: This exercise helps bring congruence to perceptions of self by self and by others. By achieving greater congruence between the way we see ourselves and the way others see us, the more likely we are to improve our relationships.

Objectives:
1. To increase self awareness.
2. To relate personal awareness, lifestyles, patterns of behavior and leisure activities.
3. To create awareness for direction in life.

Materials Needed: A pencil and a copy of the What Kind of Person Are You? guide for each participant.

Group Composition: Individual, small group, or family.

Time Required: Fifteen to 45 minutes.

Rationale: Self-esteem means how people perceive themselves. Individuals need to become aware of how they view themselves as well as how others view them. Once these two goals are accomplished, opportunities for understanding and communication are enhanced.

Procedures:
1. Hand out copies of the guide What Kind of Person are You?, to all participants. Instruct each participant to select the one "type" which best represents himself or herself.

2. Discussion may center around: the similarities and differences between individuals selecting the same type; how this affects their work, lives, leisure, social relationships, etc.; whether they would like to change and how they might go about this; etc.

Variations: This exercise may also be used to divide a very large group into smaller groups for successive activities. Because the exercise is short, it may be used as an introduction to other activities/discussions.

Ask participants to identify the type of people that are members in their group/family.

Trainer's Notes: This exercise can be very effective in identifying how group members view themselves. Although the activity does not take much time, it lends itself to rich discussion of self-concept and self-esteem.

What Kind of Person Are You?

Someone once said that there are nine types of people - Which are you?

Wheelbarrow - Will go only when pushed.

Canoe - Has to be paddled.

Kite - Will fly away unless someone holds tightly to the string.

Cat - Content only when petted.

Football - Never know which way it will bounce.

Balloon - Full of hot air, may burst at any time.

Trailer - Will go wherever pulled.

Neon Lights - Always going off and on.

Gold Watch - Open-faced, pure as gold, dependable, self-motivated.

Artwork courtesy of Laura McLachlin.

Future Contributors

If you develop an exciting, effective, structured exercise in family dynamics that you would like to share with others in the helping profession, please send it to us for consideration, using the following guidelines:

1. Your entry should be written in a format similar to those in this handbook.
2. Contributors must either guarantee that the materials they submit are not previously copyrighted or provide a copyright release.
3. When you have adapted from the work of others, please acknowledge the original source of ideas or activities.

Ron McManus, PhD, DMin
Texas Wesleyan University
1201 Wesleyan
Fort Worth, Texas 76105
(817) 531-4915
or
Glen H. Jennings, EdD
1610 Mistywood
Denton, Texas 76201
(817) 382-8437

Name Index

Subject Index